Terry Far

TEST YOUR EXECUTIVE SKILLS

Assess your potential through 50 effective quizzes

EBURY PRESS LONDON

CONTENTS
THE TESTS

Published by Ebury Press
Division of The National Magazine Company Limited
Colquhoun House
27 37 Broadwick Street
London W1V 1FR

First impression 1987
Text copyright © 1987 by Terry Farnsworth
All rights reserved. No part of this publication may
be reproduced, stored in a retrieval system, or transmitted
in any form or by any means, electronic, mechanical,
photocopying, recording, or otherwise, without
the prior permission of the copyright owner.
ISBN 0 85223 635 2 (paperback)
     0 85223 462 7 (hardback)

Edited by Suzanne Webber
Designed by Ted McCausland
Filmset by Advanced Filmsetters (Glasgow) Ltd
Printed and bound in Great Britain by
Anchor Brendon, Tiptree, Essex

─────────────────NOTE─────────────────
Throughout this book, the terms *he*, *him* and *his* have been used for
the sake of convenience and to make easier reading, and are not meant
to be taken as sexist.

ARE YOU A GOOD LEADER?

ONE

Leadership is a key management skill. It has a major impact upon the way people perform and the results they achieve.

What kind of leader are you? Answering the following questions will help you to find out.

Question One
WOULD YOU RATHER BE:

A *The spokesman for a group?* ◇

B *The captain of a team?* ◇

C *The commander of an army?* ◇

Question Two
DO YOU CONSULT YOUR SUBORDINATES BEFORE TAKING IMPORTANT DECISIONS WHICH WILL AFFECT THEIR WORK?

A *Nearly always—I value their experience.* ◇

B *Sometimes—it depends how much time I have.* ◇

C *Never—I believe a manager should manage.* ◇

Question Three
DO YOU ALLOW YOUR PEOPLE TO PARTICIPATE IN SETTING THEIR OBJECTIVES?

A *Always—I feel it's vital to get their commitment.* ◇

B *Sometimes—usually for the less important goals.* ◇

C *Never—they would simply try to persuade me to accept lower standards.* ◇

Question Four
WHAT DO YOU CONSIDER IS THE MAIN BENEFIT OF DELEGATION?

A *Makes life easier for the boss.* ◇

4 B *Helps to develop individual abilities.* ◇

C *Allows the boss to concentrate on higher-level work.* ◇

<hr>

Question Five

HOW MUCH AUTHORITY DO YOU DELEGATE TO SUBORDINATES? DO YOU PREFER THEM TO:

A *Check with you first before taking important decisions?* ◇

B *Decide for themselves whether to consult you?* ◇

C *Act first and tell you later?* ◇

<hr>

Question Six

A SUBORDINATE TURNS IN AN OUTSTANDING PERFORMANCE ON AN IMPORTANT ASSIGNMENT. WOULD YOU:

A *Congratulate him personally right away?* ◇

B *Say nothing in case he might ask for more money?* ◇

C *Congratulate him if you happened to meet him?* ◇

<hr>

Question Seven

YOU HAVE TO ANNOUNCE A VERY IMPORTANT POLICY CHANGE TO YOUR GROUP. WOULD YOU:

A *Issue a general circular, enclosing a copy of the new policy?* ◇

B *Brief one of your lieutenants and ask him to communicate with the rest of the group?* ◇

C *Call a meeting and explain the changes personally?* ◇

<hr>

Question Eight

A SUBORDINATE'S GENERAL PERFORMANCE BEGINS TO DETERIORATE SHARPLY. WOULD YOU:

A *Threaten him with tough action unless he improves quickly?* ◇

B *Discuss the problem with him to try to discover the cause?* ◇

C *Ask the personnel department to investigate?* ◇

<hr>

Question Nine

A SUBORDINATE SUGGESTS A RADICAL NEW IDEA—WHICH YOU FEEL IS UNSOUND. WOULD YOU:

A *Point out its weaknesses but encourage him to try again?* ◇

B *Tell him it's impractical/too costly/not the right time?* ◇

C *Promise to think about it and then file it?* ◇

Question Ten

ONE OF YOUR PEOPLE IS DEPRESSED AFTER MISSING A PROMOTION. WOULD YOU:

A *Tell him not to worry—everyone must expect the occasional setback?* ◇

B *Suggest what action he might take to become a stronger candidate for the next promotion vacancy?* ◇

C *Tell him the job wouldn't have suited him anyway?* ◇

ARE YOU KEEPING UP TO DATE?

test

TWO

Change is the only certainty. In tomorrow's business world executives who fail to keep up to date make it easy for companies to dispense with their services.

Are you a survivor—or a loser? Answer YES or NO to the following questions (*tick for yes, cross for no*):

1. *Have you identified what changes are likely to affect your job during the next five years?* ◇

2. *Have you drawn up plans to acquire new knowledge and skills?* ◇

3. *Do you always look for better ways of doing your job?* ◇

4. *Have you introduced at least three new ideas into your operation during the past year?* ◇

5. *Are you always on the look-out for opportunities to acquire new experience?* ◇

6. *Do you encourage your boss to delegate to you?*

7. *Are you following a systematic reading programme to keep up with new developments in your field?*

8. *Do you ever seek the help of colleagues with specialist expertise and discuss your problems with them?*

9. *Are you a member of a professional institution or management group?*

10. *Do you regularly attend its meetings?*

11. *Have you ever volunteered to give a talk on a topic which would involve you in doing some research?*

12. *Would you be willing to learn from a subordinate who possessed certain expertise which you needed?*

13. *Have you ever applied for a place on either an in-company or external training course?*

14. *Have you ever taken a correspondence course or attended evening classes in a business subject?*

15. *Have you ever published an article or given a talk on a successful innovation for which you were responsible?*

16. *Do you encourage your subordinates to keep up to date and do everything possible to help them?*

HOW SELF-CONFIDENT ARE YOU?

test
THREE

Self-confidence is the basis of any manager's performance. Not to be confused with arrogance or conceit, it provides the motivating thrust which gets results.

You may believe that you are brimming with self-confidence but is this really true? How would you handle the following situations?

WHEN A SUBJECT IS THROWN OPEN FOR DISCUSSION AT A MEETING, DO YOU:

A *Contribute your opinion as quickly as possible?* ◇

B *Stay silent unless you are asked a question?* ◇

C *Comment only after several other people have spoken?* ◇

IF YOU WERE CRITICISED UNJUSTLY BY YOUR BOSS, WOULD YOU:

A *Defend yourself forcefully, displaying considerable emotion?* ◇

B *Give your side of the story, calmly and rationally?* ◇

C *Stay quiet but inwardly seethe with resentment?* ◇

IF YOU WERE INVITED TO GIVE A TALK TO A PRESTIGIOUS NON-COMPANY AUDIENCE, WOULD YOU:

A *Decline—pleading pressure of work?* ◇

B *Accept on condition that you were given a briefing?* ◇

C *Ask for a day or two to think it over?* ◇

A FRIEND ASKS FOR YOUR SUPPORT FOR A PROPOSAL WHICH HE INTENDS TO PRESENT AT A MEETING. YOU BELIEVE HIS IDEA TO BE UNSOUND. WOULD YOU:

A *Agree to support him but then find an excuse for not attending the meeting?* ◇

B *Try to convince him to withdraw his proposal?* ◇

C *Tell him you will make up your mind after listening to the discussion at the meeting?* ◇

WHEN ENTERING A ROOM AT A COMPANY SOCIAL FUNCTION, DO YOU:

A *Look around for your friends and join them immediately?* ◇

B *Start chatting to the nearest person, even if you do not know him or her well?* ◇

C *Head straight for the bar and order a drink?* ◇

————————Question Six————————

YOU ARE PROMOTED TO RUN A DEPARTMENT WHICH WAS REPUTEDLY WELL-MANAGED AND HIGHLY EFFICIENT UNDER YOUR PREDECESSOR. WOULD YOU:

A *Immediately review all existing policies critically?* ◇

B *Let it be known that you will be making no major changes for at least six months?* ◇

C *Ask your staff to submit their ideas for improvement?* ◇

————————Question Seven————————

YOUR BOSS ASKS YOU TO UNDERTAKE AN EXTREMELY IMPORTANT SPECIAL ASSIGNMENT. FAILURE COULD SERIOUSLY DAMAGE YOUR REPUTATION AND PROSPECTS. WOULD YOU:

A *Ask him to clarify your objectives and authority?* ◇

B *Specify what resources you will require and why you will need them?* ◇

C *Seek a guarantee that you will be able to return to your old job after completing the assignment?* ◇

————————Question Eight————————

YOUR BOSS QUOTES SOME INACCURATE STATISTICS DURING A PRESENTATION AT A DEPARTMENTAL MEETING. WOULD YOU:

A *Interrupt his presentation tactfully and point out the error?* ◇

B *Query the figures when he asks for questions?* ◇

C *Tell him privately some time later?* ◇

————————Question Nine————————

YOU RETURN TO THE OFFICE FROM A SEMINAR FEELING HIGHLY ENTHUSIASTIC ABOUT A NEW MANAGEMENT TECHNIQUE. WOULD YOU:

A *Assign a subordinate to get more data on possible applications?* ◇

9

B *Try to convince the M.D. that it should be implemented across the whole company?*

C *Implement it within your own department?*

Question Ten
IF YOU WERE SELECTING A NEW SUBORDINATE, WOULD YOU CHOOSE:

A *A person who is original and inventive but rather temperamental?*

B *A person who is reliable and conscientious but lacks new ideas?*

C *A highly intelligent person with a reputation for being lazy?*

CAN YOU BUILD TEAM SPIRIT?

Team spirit is not simply a vital ingredient of success on the sports field: it is equally important in modern business, as the competitive struggle grows fiercer every year. And as technologies become more complex, many tasks require sustained effort by highly committed working groups. You may be effective in dealing with individuals but how do you rate as the leader of a team? Answer YES or NO to these questions (*tick for yes, cross for no*):

1. *Having consulted individual members of your group, have you set challenging objectives for the group as a whole, with realistic target dates and clear standards of performance?*

2. *Have you communicated these objectives at a group meeting, dealt with any questions and noted any constructive suggestions?*

3. Have you issued copies of the agreed objectives to each member of the group?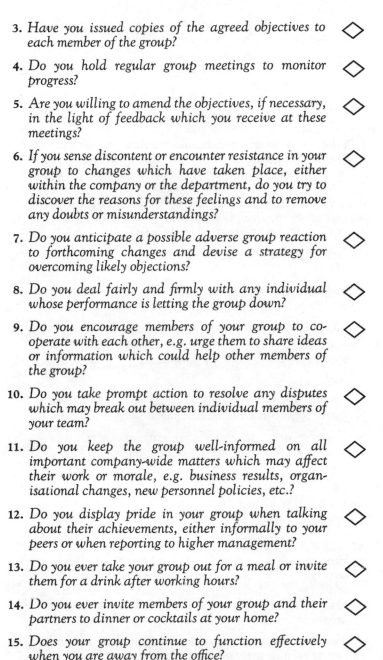

4. Do you hold regular group meetings to monitor progress?

5. Are you willing to amend the objectives, if necessary, in the light of feedback which you receive at these meetings?

6. If you sense discontent or encounter resistance in your group to changes which have taken place, either within the company or the department, do you try to discover the reasons for these feelings and to remove any doubts or misunderstandings?

7. Do you anticipate a possible adverse group reaction to forthcoming changes and devise a strategy for overcoming likely objections?

8. Do you deal fairly and firmly with any individual whose performance is letting the group down?

9. Do you encourage members of your group to co-operate with each other, e.g. urge them to share ideas or information which could help other members of the group?

10. Do you take prompt action to resolve any disputes which may break out between individual members of your team?

11. Do you keep the group well-informed on all important company-wide matters which may affect their work or morale, e.g. business results, organisational changes, new personnel policies, etc.?

12. Do you display pride in your group when talking about their achievements, either informally to your peers or when reporting to higher management?

13. Do you ever take your group out for a meal or invite them for a drink after working hours?

14. Do you ever invite members of your group and their partners to dinner or cocktails at your home?

15. Does your group continue to function effectively when you are away from the office?

DO YOU DELEGATE EFFECTIVELY?

test
FIVE*

Delegation is the lifeblood of any successful enterprise. Properly planned and executed, it means better decision-making, less red tape and more highly-motivated employees.

When delegating a challenging assignment to an inexperienced subordinate, would you—answer YES (*tick*) or NO (*cross*) to each question:

1. *Explain the assignment and spell out the objective(s)?* ◇

2. *Explain why the job is important—and how the company or department will benefit?* ◇

3. *Explain how he will benefit (broader experience, better promotion prospects, etc.)?* ◇

4. *Delegate any additional authority needed to do the job?* ◇

5. *Specify what resources have been allocated to him (money, people, equipment, etc.)?* ◇

6. *Clarify any relevant company policies and procedures which he may not know about?* ◇

7. *Check whether he needs any special training for the job?* ◇

8. *Brief him on some of the key people he will be working with—and, if possible, introduce him?* ◇

9. *Specify a target date for completion of the assignment?* ◇

10. *Explain how his performance will be measured?* ◇

11. *Fix some dates when you will meet him to review progress?* ◇

12. *Tell him what kind of information you will be expecting him to report—and in what form?* ◇

13. Check that he has understood the main points of his briefing? ◇

14. Assure him that if he gets into difficulties, you'll be glad to help him? ◇

15. Wish him good luck? ◇

ARE YOU DEVELOPING YOUR SUBORDINATES?

test
SIX

Remember, you are accountable not just for your own performance but also for the results of those who work for you. People are your most important resource and it's up to every executive to get the best possible return from his human assets.

Are you developing your staff effectively? Answer YES or NO to the following questions (*tick for yes, cross for no*):

1. Do you regularly review the training needs of your staff and identify each individual's priorities? ◇

2. Do you discuss these needs with the employee and devise an effective action plan? ◇

3. Before one of your people attends a formal training course, do you brief him as to why you are sending him and indicate what benefits he can expect from attending? ◇

4. When he returns from the course, do you discuss what he has learned and encourage him to try new ideas? ◇

5. Do you encourage your people to develop themselves and indicate some possible lines of action, e.g. studying for further qualifications, attending the meetings of professional bodies? ◇

6. Are you systematically developing them on the job, e.g. through effective delegation, setting them

13

challenging objectives, giving them opportunities to acquire new experience? ◇

7. *Do you ever encourage them to read management books or journals which you believe would help them?* ◇

8. *When establishing each individual's objectives, do you include at least one self-development objective and monitor progress at regular intervals?* ◇

9. *Do you encourage them to develop their own subordinates and include this as an objective in their performance appraisals?* ◇

10. *Have you discussed each individual's career aspirations with him and counselled him as to how best he may achieve them?* ◇

11. *Do you take time out occasionally to give your subordinates some individual coaching on specific aspects of their performance where they need to improve?* ◇

12. *Are you developing a potential successor for each key job in your group?* ◇

13. *Have you considered the greater use of job rotation both as a means of broadening the experience of your people and of reducing your vulnerability if certain individuals were to leave or be promoted?* ◇

14. *Do you ever assign an individual to carry out a special project in order to widen his experience and give him the opportunity of acquiring new skills?* ◇

15. *Do you actively encourage your staff to come up with new ideas?* ◇

HOW STATUS-CONSCIOUS ARE YOU?

SEVEN

How important is status to you? In the armed services a man's rank is displayed on his uniform: in business it is not nearly as straightforward. Cars, offices, desks—there is a whole range of objects which signify an executive's place in the pecking order.

In many organisations executives of different rank are encouraged to 'know their place'; in others a more relaxed atmosphere exists.

Question One

DO YOUR SUBORDINATES ADDRESS YOU:

A *By your title (Mr/Mrs/Ms/Miss)?* ◇

B *By your first name?* ◇

Question Two

ASSUMING YOU HAVE A CHOICE, DO YOU USUALLY LUNCH IN:

A *The executive dining room, with your peers?* ◇

B *The staff restaurant, with your subordinates?* ◇

Question Three

IF YOUR COMPANY BUILT A NEW CAR PARK FOR EMPLOYEES, WOULD YOU:

A *Fight tooth and nail for a reserved space?* ◇

B *Be content to park anywhere?* ◇

Question Four

DO YOU VALUE A LARGE OFFICE BECAUSE:

A *It shows your importance in the organisation?* ◇

B *It enables you to hold small meetings?* ◇

Question Five

A SUBORDINATE MENTIONS THAT HE HAS HAD A PERSONAL DISCUSSION WITH YOUR BOSS. WOULD YOU:

A *Reprimand him for going over your head?* ◇

B *Find out why he did so and what happened?* ◇

Question Six

YOUR BOSS TELEPHONES YOU WITH A MINOR, NON-URGENT REQUEST. WOULD YOU:

A *Drop everything and give it top priority?* ◇ 15

B *Let it take its turn with other similar jobs?* ◇

Question Seven

WHAT KIND OF MATERIAL DO YOU PUT ON DISPLAY IN YOUR OFFICE. IS IT:

A *Mainly prestigious—degrees, diplomas, certificates, photographs of you attending important functions?* ◇

B *Mainly domestic—pictures of your partner and family?* ◇

Question Eight

A SUBORDINATE INVITES YOU TO GO FOR A DRINK AT THE END OF A GRUELLING DAY. WOULD YOU:

A *Decline, saying that you've promised your partner to get home early?* ◇

B *Say 'What a great idea!' and accept?* ◇

Question Nine

AS AN ECONOMY MEASURE, YOUR COMPANY DECIDES THAT SENIOR EXECUTIVES SHOULD HENCEFORTH BE PROVIDED WITH MEDIUM-SIZED CARS INSTEAD OF THE TRADITIONAL LARGE, PRESTIGE MODELS. WOULD YOU:

A *Feel outraged and start looking for another job?* ◇

B *Start working out how much you would be saving on your private petrol?* ◇

Question Ten

YOUR OFFICE BOOKCASE IS CRAMMED WITH BOOKS ON MANAGEMENT. IS THIS BECAUSE:

A *You wish to impress your boss and important visitors?* ◇

B *You believe in keeping up to date?* ◇

Question Eleven

AT THE OFFICE PARTY YOU SEE THAT NEITHER YOUR FAITHFUL SECRETARY NOR YOUR BOSS'S WIFE IS DANCING. WHO WOULD YOU ASK TO DANCE FIRST:

A *Your boss's wife?* ◇

16 **B** *Your secretary?* ◇

Question Twelve
A SUBORDINATE TRIES TO INTEREST YOU IN HIS HOLIDAY SNAPS. DO YOU:

A *Say 'Leave them with me and I'll look at them later'?* ◇

B *Look at them admiringly and congratulate him upon his skill?* ◇

Question Thirteen
YOU DECIDE TO HOLD A MEETING AT A CITY HOTEL. DO YOU:

A *Pick the most luxurious hotel in town in order to impress those attending?* ◇

B *Select the one with the best value-for-money conference package?* ◇

Question Fourteen
A SUBORDINATE REFERS TO THE CHAIRMAN BY HIS NICKNAME. DO YOU:

A *Insist that in future he should show more respect?* ◇

B *Ignore it?* ◇

Question Fifteen
WHEN HAVING A MEETING WITH A SUBORDINATE, DO YOU:

A *Always remain seated behind your desk?* ◇

B *Come out from behind your desk and sit nearer to him?* ◇

Question Sixteen
THE CHAIRMAN INVITES YOU TO SPEND A WEEKEND AT HIS COUNTRY HOME. DO YOU:

A *Make sure that all your colleagues and subordinates know about it?* ◇

B *Regard it as a private matter and keep it to yourself?* ◇

Do You Appraise People Fairly?

EIGHT

Appraising the performance of a subordinate is one of the executive's most responsible tasks—one which often has a considerable impact upon the employee's pay and promotion prospects, as well as upon his personal motivation. What's more, conducting a constructive appraisal discussion provides a searching test of a boss's skills in personal relations.

How effectively do you appraise your people?

Question One

WHAT DO YOU BELIEVE IS THE MAIN PURPOSE OF PERFORMANCE APPRAISAL? IS IT:

A *To give the employee feedback on his past performance?* ◇

B *To criticise him for his shortcomings?* ◇

C *To motivate him to do a better job in the future?* ◇

Question Two

SHOULD AN EMPLOYEE BE APPRAISED:

A *On his knowledge, skills and attitudes, regardless of his short-term results?* ◇

B *Strictly according to his results?* ◇

C *On a mixture of both his abilities and his results?* ◇

Question Three

WHAT WOULD BE THE MOST USEFUL DATA TO CONSULT WHEN WRITING A SUBORDINATE'S APPRAISAL:

A *His job description?* ◇

B *His attendance records, expense claims, etc.?* ◇

C *His previous performance appraisal form?* ◇

Question Four

IF A SUBORDINATE'S PERFORMANCE BEGAN TO

DETERIORATE AND HIS FORMAL APPRAISAL WAS
NOT DUE FOR SEVERAL MONTHS, WOULD YOU:

A *Turn a blind eye and hope that it would soon improve?* ◇

B *Discuss the situation with him and agree upon an improvement plan?* ◇

C *Make a note of any shortcomings in order to raise them with him at the appraisal interview?* ◇

—————————————Question Five—————————————
IF A SUBORDINATE BECAME HIGHLY EMOTIONAL
DURING A DISCUSSION OF HIS PERFORMANCE,
WOULD YOU:

A *Listen to him carefully without interrupting?* ◇

B *End the interview to give him a chance to calm down?* ◇

C *Rebuke him for losing his self-control?* ◇

—————————————Question Six—————————————
WHEN PLANNING AN APPRAISAL INTERVIEW,
WHAT KIND OF STRATEGY WOULD YOU USE?
WOULD YOU:

A *Start by discussing the individual's strengths and then deal with his weaknesses?* ◇

B *Start with his weaknesses and then deal with his strengths?* ◇

C *Start and finish with some strengths and deal with his weaknesses in the middle?* ◇

—————————————Question Seven—————————————
EMPLOYEES IN THE PRIVATE SECTOR GENERALLY
EXPECT THEIR PAY TO BE INFLUENCED BY THEIR
PERFORMANCE APPRAISALS. WOULD YOU TELL AN
EMPLOYEE WHAT SALARY INCREASE HE WOULD
BE GETTING:

A *During the appraisal interview?* ◇

B *At a separate discussion on salary matters?* ◇

C *By letter as and when you had decided what the increase should be?* ◇

—————————————Question Eight—————————————
FOLLOWING A DISCUSSION OF A SUBORDINATE'S   19

WEAKNESSES DURING AN APPRAISAL INTERVIEW,
WOULD YOU:

A *Agree a plan by which both you and he would commit yourselves to specific actions to help him improve?* ◇

B *Warn him that failure to improve could jeopardise his salary and promotion prospects?* ◇

C *Spell out some specific actions which he himself should take?* ◇

———————————Question Nine———————————

AT THE CONCLUSION OF THE APPRAISAL
INTERVIEW, WOULD YOU:

A *Allow the employee to read his appraisal and to add any written comments he may wish to make?* ◇

B *Not allow him to read it but ask for his comments and record them yourself?* ◇

C *Neither allow him to read it nor ask for his comments?* ◇

———————————Question Ten———————————

DO YOU BELIEVE THAT IN GENERAL APPRAISALS
SHOULD BE WRITTEN:

A *Only when subordinates request them?* ◇

B *On a regular time-scale, e.g. once a year?* ◇

C *Only when the subordinate's performance begins to deteriorate?* ◇

DO YOU KNOW WHAT'S HAPPENING IN THE OUTSIDE WORLD?

Only companies and executives who can adapt to change are likely to survive in the new technological age.

Are you in touch with new developments and new techniques? Here's a chance to check your knowledge.

Question One
WOULD YOU FORM A QUALITY CIRCLE TO:

A *Select employees for senior management jobs?* ◇

B *Ask employees to generate ideas for improvements?* ◇

C *Assist you in determining long-range strategies?* ◇

Question Two
WHAT IS THE 'BOSTON EFFECT'?

A *A personality test that measures resistance to stress.* ◇

B *A method of categorising products and services.* ◇

C *A statistical technique used in inventory control.* ◇

Question Three
HOW WOULD YOU USE 'POSITIVE REINFORCEMENT'?

A *Allocating more resources to high-growth activities.* ◇

B *Improving the organisation's public image.* ◇

C *Recognising good performance by individuals or groups.* ◇

Question Four
WHAT IS 'SYNECTICS'?

A *A creative problem-solving technique.* ◇

B *A branch of laser technology used in glass manufacture.* ◇

C *A method of forecasting retail sales.* ◇

Question Five
WHO WROTE THE BEST-SELLING BOOK QUALITY IS FREE?

A *Peter Drucker.* ◇

B *Philip Crosby.* ◇

C *Yukio Mishima.* ◇

Question Six
WHICH TYPES OF COMPUTER ARE LIKELY TO HAVE

THE HIGHEST SALES GROWTH DURING THE 1980s?

A *General-purpose computers.* ◇

B *Minicomputers.* ◇

C *Desktop computers.* ◇

————————————*Question Seven*————————————

WHICH COMPUTER LANGUAGE WOULD YOU BE
MOST LIKELY TO LEARN IN ORDER TO
PROGRAMME YOUR PERSONAL COMPUTER?

A *PL/1.* ◇

B *Basic.* ◇

C *Fortran.* ◇

————————————*Question Eight*————————————

WHAT IS THE NO. 1 OBJECTIVE OF MOST LARGE
JAPANESE COMPANIES?

A *High market share.* ◇

B *Maximum profit.* ◇

C *Excellent employee relations.* ◇

————————————*Question Nine*————————————

THE BOOK *THE THIRD WAVE* DESCRIBES THE KIND
OF SOCIETY THAT WILL RESULT FROM THE
INFLUENCE OF NEW TECHNOLOGIES. WHO WROTE
IT?

A *Herman Kahn.* ◇

B *Alvin Toffler.* ◇

C *E. F. Schumacher.* ◇

————————————*Question Ten*————————————

HOW WOULD YOU USE 'TRANSACTIONAL
ANALYSIS'?

A *Forecasting potential bad debts.* ◇

B *Improving communication and personal relation-* ◇
ships.

C *Identifying companies as acquisition prospects.* ◇

————————————*Question Eleven*————————————

WHICH OF THE FOLLOWING TYPES OF WORK IS

LIKELY TO PROVIDE THE GREATEST
OPPORTUNITIES FOR THE USE OF INDUSTRIAL
ROBOTS?

A *Assembly work.* ◇

B *Handling soft goods, e.g. the garment and shoe* ◇
industries.

C *Packaging and package distribution.* ◇

———————————Question Twelve———————————
WHAT IS THE MOST IMPORTANT CAPABILITY
WHICH THE MORE ADVANCED ROBOTS OF THE
FUTURE WILL NEED?

A *Improved sense of vision.* ◇

B *Better tactile sensing.* ◇

C *Greater mobility.* ◇

———————————Question Thirteen———————————
WHO WAS THE FAMOUS WRITER WHO DEVISED
'THE THREE LAWS OF ROBOTICS'?

A *Kurt Vonnegut.* ◇

B *Erich von Daniken.* ◇

C *Isaac Asimov.* ◇

———————————Question Fourteen———————————
WHAT IS SCIMITAR?

A *A systematic approach to new product development.* ◇

B *A computerised production control system.* ◇

C *A linear programming technique used by Japanese* ◇
companies for controlling suppliers.

———————————Question Fifteen———————————
WHAT DO YOU PLAN TO DO TO FILL ANY GAPS IN
YOUR KNOWLEDGE REVEALED BY THIS TEST?

A *I'll hire a top-flight consultant to advise me.* ◇

B *Nothing—I'll wait until I'm sure I know what I need.* ◇

C *As a first step I'll read some books on each subject.* ◇ 23

DO YOU PROCRASTINATE?

Do you delay? Do you put off until tomorrow things you should do today? Ask yourself the following questions.

1. *Do I invent reasons and look for excuses for not acting on a tough problem?*

   Frequently ◇   Sometimes ◇   Rarely ◇   Never ◇

2. *Does it take pressure to get me working on a difficult assignment?*

   Frequently ◇   Sometimes ◇   Rarely ◇   Never ◇

3. *Do I take half measures which will avoid or delay unpleasant or difficult action?*

   Frequently ◇   Sometimes ◇   Rarely ◇   Never ◇

4. *Do I allow too many interruptions and crises that interfere with my accomplishing important tasks?*

   Frequently ◇   Sometimes ◇   Rarely ◇   Never ◇

5. *Do I avoid forthright answers when pressed for an unpleasant decision?*

   Frequently ◇   Sometimes ◇   Rarely ◇   Never ◇

6. *Have I been guilty of neglecting follow-up aspects of important action plans?*

   Frequently ◇   Sometimes ◇   Rarely ◇   Never ◇

7. *Do I try to get other people to do unpleasant assignments for me?*

   Frequently ◇   Sometimes ◇   Rarely ◇   Never ◇

8. *Do I schedule important or difficult jobs too late in the day, or constantly take them home to do in the evening?*

   Frequently ◇   Sometimes ◇   Rarely ◇   Never ◇

9. *Do I insist upon clearing my desk of all minor and routine tasks before commencing a tough job?*

   Frequently ◇   Sometimes ◇   Rarely ◇   Never ◇

10. When pressed for a decision, do I plead for 'more time to think'?

Frequently ◇   Sometimes ◇   Rarely ◇   Never ◇

11. Do I use minor ailments as an excuse to stay away from the office when unpopular decisions need to be taken?

Frequently ◇   Sometimes ◇   Rarely ◇   Never ◇

12. When dealing with my mail, do I keep on picking up pieces of paper and putting them down again without taking some kind of action?

Frequently ◇   Sometimes ◇   Rarely ◇   Never ◇

13. Do I allow meetings to end without decisions being taken because I am afraid to offend a powerful individual or faction?

Frequently ◇   Sometimes ◇   Rarely ◇   Never ◇

14. Do I blame my boss for my own indecisiveness by saying 'He's never around when I want to discuss something with him'?

Frequently ◇   Sometimes ◇   Rarely ◇   Never ◇

15. Do I form committees, task forces and working parties to provide me with further information—even though I have enough already?

Frequently ◇   Sometimes ◇   Rarely ◇   Never ◇

CAN YOU MANAGE OUTSTANDING PEOPLE?

test
ELEVEN

Outstanding people are worth their weight in gold to any organisation, but they can sometimes be difficult to manage. Thrusting and creative, they are often impatient of rules and regulations and seek opportunities to 'do their own thing'.

25

Too much control and they will almost certainly leave; too little and they will be resented by their colleagues. How do you manage a high-flyer? Do you:

———————————————Question One———————————————

A *Regard him as a challenge to your management skills?* ◇

B *View him as a threat to your own security?* ◇

———————————————Question Two———————————————

A *Leave him to guess what he is expected to achieve?* ◇

B *Set him clear objectives and challenging deadlines?* ◇

———————————————Question Three———————————————

A *See him only infrequently because you are 'too busy'?* ◇

B *Make time to discuss his ideas and suggestions?* ◇

———————————————Question Four———————————————

A *Challenge his ideas and be constructively critical?* ◇

B *Display indifference and be negative or carping?* ◇

———————————————Question Five———————————————

A *Make him constantly aware of your senior status?* ◇

B *Treat him as a valued member of your team?* ◇

———————————————Question Six———————————————

A *Praise him promptly for outstanding achievement?* ◇

B *Ignore his achievements (or try to steal the credit)?* ◇

———————————————Question Seven———————————————

A *See that his salary reflects his extra contribution?* ◇

B *Reward him very much the same as everyone else?* ◇

———————————————Question Eight———————————————

A *Ask for his ideas and suggestions on some of your own work problems?* ◇

B *Promptly discourage him when he shows any interest?* ◇

—————————————Question Nine—————————————

A Nominate him for courses which would assist his development? ◇

B Deny him opportunities in case he should appear more knowledgeable than you? ◇

—————————————Question Ten—————————————

A Keep pressurising him for reports which you promptly file? ◇

B Request only those reports which you really need? ◇

—————————————Question Eleven—————————————

A Make a point of appraising him regularly? ◇

B Wait until he asks for an appraisal? ◇

—————————————Question Twelve—————————————

A Discuss his career goals with him and help him to devise a plan for achieving them? ◇

B Become vague or unhelpful when he seeks your guidance? ◇

—————————————Question Thirteen—————————————

A Rarely discuss his progress and achievements with your boss? ◇

B Take pride in reporting how well he is developing? ◇

—————————————Question Fourteen—————————————

A Ensure that he is nominated for relevant promotion vacancies outside your own group? ◇

B Fail to nominate him because you don't want to lose him? ◇

—————————————Question Fifteen—————————————

A Reprimand him sharply if he upsets any of his colleagues? ◇

B Show him how he can achieve his goals by being more tactful? ◇

ARE YOU WELL ORGANISED?

TWELVE

Few things do more to undermine an executive's credibility than a reputation for being badly organised. Bad working habits can only lead to a loss of respect from your boss and/or the people who work for you.

The key to organising others is to be well organised yourself. Answer YES or NO to these questions (*tick for yes, cross for no*):

1. *Do you have a plan for how you will spend your day when you arrive at the office?*

2. *Do you give priority to the things that must be done rather than the things you like to do?*

3. *Do you have a regular time each day for dealing with correspondence?*

4. *Do you deal with most of your mail on the day that it arrives?*

5. *Do you know what time of day you work most effectively, and therefore use this for working on your most difficult tasks?*

6. *Do you keep your desk clear of all papers except those on which you are working?*

7. *Do you set aside a period of time each day to make important outside telephone calls?*

8. *Before telephoning, do you make notes on all the key points you want to cover?*

9. *Do you make full use of your diary for noting dates, times, places, names, addresses, telephone numbers, etc.?*

10. *Do you have an efficient reminder system?*

11. *Do you devise effective procedures for dealing with routine work?*

12. *Do you know which papers are in which drawers of your desk?*

13. *Do you have an efficient filing system?*

14. *Do you cut off your telephone during important meetings rather than suffer constant interruptions?*

15. *Do you let your secretary know where you can be contacted if you leave your office for an unscheduled meeting?*

CAN YOU RUN EFFECTIVE MEETINGS?

THIRTEEN

Meetings are an important part of every executive's life. Whether their purpose is to solve problems or to generate ideas, they play a key role in the communications process.

Running effective meetings provides yet another challenge to the executive's leadership skills—one which exposes them to searching public scrutiny. Many a career has been made or broken by an executive's performance in this area.

Suppose that you have called a meeting of about six of your subordinates in order to solve an urgent problem which has been assigned to you by your boss. How would you deal with the following situations?

Question One

HOW WOULD YOU OPEN THE MEETING? WOULD YOU:

A *Plunge straight into a detailed explanation of the problem?*

B *State the problem briefly and then throw it open for discussion?*

29

C *State the problem briefly, explain why it is important and spell out what you are expecting the meeting to achieve?* ◇

Question Two

ASSUMING THAT THERE IS SOMEONE IN THE GROUP WHO HAS EXPERT KNOWLEDGE OF THE PROBLEM, WOULD YOU:

A *Invite him to contribute his views right away?* ◇

B *Hold him in reserve until others have spoken?* ◇

C *Leave him to contribute as and when he chooses?* ◇

Question Three

A HEATED EXCHANGE OF VIEWS BETWEEN TWO INDIVIDUALS THREATENS TO WRECK THE MEETING. WOULD YOU:

A *Rebuke both of them and move on to a new point?* ◇

B *Let them fight it out and back whichever view wins majority support?* ◇

C *Thank both individuals for their comments, give your decision and move on to the next point?* ◇

Question Four

A NOTORIOUSLY VERBOSE INDIVIDUAL CONSTANTLY SLOWS THE MEETING DOWN WITH HIS LENGTHY CONTRIBUTIONS, MOST OF WHICH ARE EITHER IRRELEVANT OR HIGHLY THEORETICAL. WOULD YOU:

A *Tell him sharply that you've heard enough from him and must now hear from others?* ◇

B *Interrupt him tactfully and point out that time is limited?* ◇

C *Ignore him and hope that others will deal with him?* ◇

Question Five

A MEMBER OF THE MEETING, AN INTELLIGENT BUT RATHER TIMID INDIVIDUAL, HAS SO FAR REMAINED SILENT. WOULD YOU:

A *Assume that he has nothing to contribute?* ◇

30 B *Point out that you haven't heard from him yet?* ◇

C *Ask him gently 'How do you feel about this?'?* ◇

—————————————Question Six—————————————
DURING THE MEETING YOU HEAR MANY OPINIONS
EXPRESSED WITH WHICH YOU DISAGREE. DO YOU:

A *Voice your disagreements only occasionally—* ◇
choosing only major issues?

B *Stay silent so as not to influence the other members?* ◇

C *Contribute frequently to the discussion, expressing* ◇
both your approval and disapproval of others' views?

—————————————Question Seven—————————————
AS THE DISCUSSION BECOMES INCREASINGLY
LIVELY, YOU REALISE THAT SEVERAL ISSUES ARE
BEING DISCUSSED AT THE SAME TIME. HOW
WOULD YOU REGAIN CONTROL? WOULD YOU:

A *Pound the table and call for order?* ◇

B *Summarise the discussion on the main issue and* ◇
indicate that the other items will be discussed later in
the meeting?

C *Suggest that the meeting takes a short break for coffee?* ◇

—————————————Question Eight—————————————
ASSUMING THAT THE PROBLEM UNDER
DISCUSSION IS HIGHLY COMPLEX, REQUIRING A
NUMBER OF DECISIONS ON VARIOUS ISSUES,
WOULD YOU:

A *Wait until the end of the meeting before announcing* ◇
your decisions?

B *Circulate a list of your decisions a day or so after the* ◇
meeting?

C *Throughout the meeting, after each issue has been* ◇
discussed, give your decision, allocate responsibilities
to specific individuals and set deadlines for action?

—————————————Question Nine—————————————
DURING A LONG AND COMPLEX MEETING, IT IS
ESSENTIAL THAT NOTES ARE TAKEN OF DECISIONS
AND ACTION POINTS. WOULD YOU:

A *Delegate note-taking to one of the members of the* ◇
meeting?

31

B *Do it yourself?* ◇

C *Bring your secretary to the meeting and get her to do it?* ◇

---Question Ten---

HOW WOULD YOU CONCLUDE THE MEETING? WOULD YOU:

A *Thank everyone for their contributions and set a date for a follow-up meeting to review progress?* ◇

B *Close the meeting with a perfunctory thank you and say 'Let's now get back to work'?* ◇

C *Ask everyone to stay behind to discuss another matter which has occurred to you during the meeting?* ◇

ARE YOU A GOOD SPEAKER?

---FOURTEEN---

Effective speaking is one of the really critical executive skills. Whether they are speaking at a company meeting or to an outside audience, managers are expected to be able to present their ideas in a clear and convincing manner. For good or ill, an executive's speaking abilities can have a profound impact upon his image and career prospects.

Assume that you are speaking to a group of about thirty people.

---Question One---

WHEN DECIDING UPON THE OBJECTIVES OF YOUR TALK, WOULD YOU:

A *Find out how much the audience knows about the subject and tailor your presentation to meet their needs?* ◇

B *Concentrate on meeting the needs of the most senior executive present?* ◇

C *Select those aspects of the subject which you find most interesting?* ◇

Question Two

WHEN DELIVERING YOUR PRESENTATION, WOULD YOU:

A Read from a full script so as to avoid 'drying up' or sudden forgetfulness? ◇

B Speak from just a few main headings? ◇

C Speak without notes, hoping that 'it will be all right on the night'? ◇

Question Three

HOW WOULD YOU BEGIN YOUR PRESENTATION? WOULD YOU:

A Tell them that you hope they won't find it too boring? ◇

B Apologise for any deficiencies in your speaking abilities? ◇

C State your objective and outline the main areas you intend to cover? ◇

Question Four

ASSUMING THAT YOU ARE SPEAKING IN A FAIRLY LARGE ROOM, WITHOUT A MICROPHONE, HOW WOULD YOU ENSURE THAT YOU COULD BE HEARD? WOULD YOU:

A Ask the audience in general 'Can you hear me?'? ◇

B Ask someone sitting at the back of the room? ◇

C Talk normally and assume that if someone can't hear you, he will tell you? ◇

Question Five

ASSUME THAT MOST OF THE AUDIENCE KNOW LITTLE ABOUT YOUR SUBJECT. WHAT EFFECT WOULD THIS HAVE UPON YOUR CHOICE OF WORDS? WOULD YOU:

A Use simple words and phrases known to all? ◇

B Use a large number of technical terms to impress them with your knowledge and qualifications? ◇

C Issue a glossary of technical terms at the start of your talk and encourage them to use it if they have any difficulties? ◇

Question Six

AS REGARDS THE SPEED AT WHICH YOU SPEAK, WOULD YOU:

A *Maintain a consistent speed, whether fast or slow?* ◇

B *Vary your speed but slow down when emphasising major points?* ◇

C *Not worry about it—just do what comes naturally?* ◇

Question Seven

TONE OF VOICE IS AN IMPORTANT FACTOR IN SPEAKING. WOULD YOU:

A *Keep to the same tone so that people get used to your voice?* ◇

B *Keep your tone flat and unemotional because it makes you sound more 'objective' and 'professional'?* ◇

C *Vary your tone, trying to sound as natural as possible while attempting to convey your interest and enthusiasm?* ◇

Question Eight

HOW IMPORTANT IS IT TO MAINTAIN GOOD EYE-CONTACT WITH THE AUDIENCE? WOULD YOU:

A *Look around frequently at the audience?* ◇

B *Avoid looking at them in case some people should appear to be bored or disinterested?* ◇

C *Look only at those who seem interested?* ◇

Question Nine

HOW DO YOU FEEL ABOUT USING VISUAL AIDS? WOULD YOU:

A *Use them as much as possible ('one picture is worth a thousand words')?* ◇

B *Use them as little as possible or not at all ('they distract the audience and are more trouble than they are worth')?* ◇

C *Use them selectively to clarify points which would be difficult to explain through words alone (e.g. showing and interpreting figures, illustrating how equipment or machinery works)?* ◇

Question Ten
HOW DO YOU FEEL ABOUT THE USE OF GESTURES? WOULD YOU:

A *Use them sparingly to give special emphasis to a few major points?* ◇

B *Avoid them, feeling that they make a speaker look ridiculous?* ◇

C *Do what comes naturally and allow your enthusiasm to show?* ◇

Question Eleven
HOW DO YOU FEEL ABOUT USING HUMOUR? WOULD YOU:

A *Use it as much as possible, believing that it relaxes the audience?* ◇

B *Avoid it like the plague, believing that it undermines the seriousness of your message?* ◇

C *Use it sparingly, relying upon spontaneous responses and asides rather than set-piece jokes?* ◇

Question Twelve
HOW WOULD YOU FINISH OFF YOUR PRESENTATION? WOULD YOU:

A *Summarise the main points and end with a thought-provoking punch-line?* ◇

B *Say 'That's all I have to say'—and stop?* ◇

C *Say 'Thank you for listening'—and stop?* ◇

Question Thirteen
IF YOU WERE PROVIDING HANDOUTS TO BACK UP YOUR PRESENTATION, WOULD YOU:

A *Give them out before your talk?* ◇

B *Give them to the audience during the talk and continue talking while they look at them?* ◇

C *Give them out after the talk—having told the audience during your introduction that handouts will be provided and that note-taking is unnecessary?* ◇

HOW CREATIVE ARE YOU?

FIFTEEN

Successful executives are expected to change things—
and that means coming up with new ideas. As firms
struggle for survival in overcrowded markets, human
creativity becomes more precious than ever, the factor
which determines success or failure. And yet everyone has
the ability to be creative: it's not a quality which is
confined to an intellectual élite.

Are you creative? Do the test and face the truth (*tick for yes,
cross for no*).

1. *Are you constantly on the look-out for new ideas?* ◇

2. *Do you get bored with doing things in the same old
   way?* ◇

3. *Do you get satisfaction from making improvements?* ◇

4. *Are you afraid of making mistakes?* ◇

5. *Do you worry about appearing foolish?* ◇

6. *Do you enjoy playing around with ideas?* ◇

7. *Do you resent criticism of your ideas?* ◇

8 *Do you welcome other people's ideas?* ◇

9. *Do you like solving problems in unorthodox ways?* ◇

10. *Do you give up early when you run into difficulties?* ◇

11. *Are you discouraged from acting because of lack of
    resources?* ◇

12. *Have you too much respect for traditional methods?* ◇

13. *Do you prefer a quiet life to a challenge?* ◇

14. *Do you feel that it's not your job to be critical of
    established practice?* ◇

15. *Do you fear new situations with unpredictable
    consequences?* ◇

16. *Do you mistrust your own or other people's intuition?* ◇

17. *Do you find it hard to accept disorder and confusion?* ◇

18. *Do you dislike complexity?* ◇

19. *Are you afraid of being looked upon as pushy?* ◇

20. *Are you reluctant to express your opinions?* ◇

21. *Are you afraid of having your ideas ridiculed?* ◇

22. *Are you easily discouraged by hostile criticism?* ◇

23. *Do you have difficulty in thinking broadly?* ◇

24. *Are you quick to point out why an idea won't work?* ◇

25. *Do you set yourself specific innovation objectives?* ◇

26. *Do you keep abreast of new ideas in your field?* ◇

27. *Do you encourage your subordinates to be creative?* ◇

28. *Do you ever hold meetings of your group to thrash out problems?* ◇

29. *Do you encourage your subordinates to exchange ideas?* ◇

30. *Do you promote a congenial, relaxed atmosphere in your group in which creativity can flourish?* ◇

31. *Do you make it clear that you place a high value on creativity?* ◇

32. *Do you recognise the contributions of creative individuals and reward them accordingly?* ◇

33. *Do you encourage your subordinates to work with people in other groups in order to develop new approaches?* ◇

34. *Do you encourage them to get help from wherever they need it?* ◇

35. *Do you help to promote their ideas in other parts of the organisation?* ◇

36. *Do you bring their ideas to the attention of higher management?* ◇

37. *Do you protect them against people who try to block them?* ◇

38. *Do you cultivate creative people both within and outside your own organisation?* ◇

39. *Do you ever bring in such people to address your group?* ◇

40. *Have you implemented at least six new ideas in your operation during the past year?* ◇

HOW WELL DO YOU KNOW YOUR SUBORDINATES?

SIXTEEN

Motivating subordinates to give of their best is a key executive responsibility—and this means knowing what makes them tick. People aren't just pawns to be moved about at the boss's whim: they need to be treated as *individuals* if they are to be welded into a winning team.

How well do you know the people who report to you? For each individual, photocopy the test below and write in the answers to the following questions:

1. *What is his full name?*

2. *How old is he?*

3. *What is his highest educational qualification?*

4. *If he holds a degree, what was the subject and what class was he awarded?*

5. *Which university did he attend?*

6. *Has he attained any other qualification since leaving full-time education?*

7. Has he served in the Armed Forces? In which service?

8. What previous jobs did he hold before joining the company?

9. Has he ever worked overseas? In which countries?

10. When did he join the company?

11. What jobs did he do before joining your department?

12. When did he join your department?

13. How long has he been doing his current job?

14. What was his last performance appraisal rating?

15. What is his current salary?

16. What are his ambitions (a) short-term? (b) long-term?

17. Is he undertaking any kind of private study to further his ambitions?

18. Is he prepared to relocate to gain additional experience?

19. If married, what is his wife's name?

20. Have you met his wife socially?

21. How many children does he have?

22. What are his favourite sports?

23. Has he ever achieved any sporting distinction?

24. Does he have any favourite cultural interests?

25. *Does he have any hobbies?*

26. *What kind of books does he read?*

27. *What kind of holidays does he prefer?*

28. *Does he take any regular form of exercise?*

29. *Does he have any strongly-held beliefs—political, social, religious, etc.?*

30. *Has he achieved distinction in any activity outside his job, e.g. published books or articles, addressed prestigious conferences, raised substantial funds for charity, etc.?*

ARE YOU SUFFERING FROM STRESS?

test

SEVENTEEN

The challenge of a new job, the pressure of a deadline, the battle to win a contract against fierce competition—here are examples of stressful situations which bring out the best in any thrusting executive. But when stress becomes excessive—and the breaking-point is different for each individual—an executive ceases to function effectively and it may be time to seek professional help.

The problem is to know when you may be crossing the border between healthy and unhealthy levels of stress.

These questions will help you to recognise the signs.

1. *Do you dread going to work?*

    Frequently ◇   Sometimes ◇   Never ◇

2. *Are you bored with your job?*

    Frequently ◇   Sometimes ◇   Never ◇

3. *Do you ever feel that you chose the wrong career?*

Frequently ◇   Sometimes ◇   Never ◇

4. *Do you get irritable and lose your temper easily?*

Frequently ◇   Sometimes ◇   Never ◇

5. *Do you take tranquillisers to help you get through the day?*

Frequently ◇   Sometimes ◇   Never ◇

6. *Do you ever have a lunchtime drink to 'steady your nerves'?*

Frequently ◇   Sometimes ◇   Never ◇

7. *Do you feel that your colleagues are laughing at you behind your back?*

Frequently ◇   Sometimes ◇   Never ◇

8. *Do you suspect your subordinates of plotting against you?*

Frequently ◇   Sometimes ◇   Never ◇

9. *Do you suspect your subordinates of wasting their time when you are not at the office to supervise them?*

Frequently ◇   Sometimes ◇   Never ◇

10. *Do you suspect that your boss is out to get you?*

Frequently ◇   Sometimes ◇   Never ◇

11. *Do you feel that your work is not appreciated?*

Frequently ◇   Sometimes ◇   Never ◇

12. *Do you feel that the promotion system in your organisation is grossly unfair?*

Frequently ◇   Sometimes ◇   Never ◇

13. *Do you find yourself resisting attempts to bring in changes at work?*

Frequently ◇   Sometimes ◇   Never ◇

14. *Do you ever feel trapped in your job?*

Frequently ◇   Sometimes ◇   Never ◇

15. *Do you lie awake at night worrying about your problems at work?*

Frequently ◇   Sometimes ◇   Never ◇

16. *Do you ever feel like resigning from your job and starting a new life in a completely different environment?*

Frequently ◇   Sometimes ◇   Never ◇

17. *Do you suffer quite severe bouts of depression?*

Frequently ◇   Sometimes ◇   Never ◇

18. *Do you ever find yourself shouting at people on television who express views with which you strongly disagree?*

Frequently ◇   Sometimes ◇   Never ◇

19. *Do you feel isolated and alone in the world?*

Frequently ◇   Sometimes ◇   Never ◇

20. *Do you ever contemplate suicide?*

Frequently ◇   Sometimes ◇   Never ◇

CAN YOU HANDLE A CRISIS?

---EIGHTEEN---

There are many occasions in an executive's life when things go badly wrong and he finds himself facing a crisis. Sometimes the issues involved are relatively trivial, at other times they can have a decisive impact upon his career. But large or small, what really matters is how he handles them—whether he can identify the problem, make the right choices and act decisively.

Here are some situations which you might one day have to deal with. How would you cope?

---*Question One*---

YOU HAVE ORGANISED A MAJOR COMPANY CONFERENCE. THIRTY MINUTES BEFORE HE IS DUE TO APPEAR YOUR OPENING SPEAKER TELEPHONES

TO SAY THAT HIS CAR HAS BROKEN DOWN FIVE MILES FROM THE VENUE. WOULD YOU:

A *Re-schedule his presentation so that he appears later in the programme?* ◇

B *Delay the opening of the conference for 30 minutes and send a taxi to collect him?* ◇

C *Delay the conference and pick him up yourself?* ◇

―――――――――Question Two―――――――――

YOU ARE WAITING AT THE AIRPORT TO MEET A VIP VISITOR AND DRIVE HIM TO THE OFFICE. AS HE EMERGES FROM CUSTOMS YOU SEE THAT HE IS NOTICEABLY THE WORSE FOR DRINK. DO YOU:

A *Say nothing and hope that he begins to sober up on the way to the office?* ◇

B *Suggest that you take him to his hotel to check in and to 'freshen up'?* ◇

C *Insist upon driving him to the hotel and see that he goes to bed?* ◇

―――――――――Question Three―――――――――

YOU ENTER A COLLEAGUE'S OFFICE TO FIND HIM TEETERING ON THE WINDOW LEDGE AND THREATENING TO JUMP. BELOW HIM IS A 50-FOOT DROP. WOULD YOU:

A *Rush over and try to pull him in?* ◇

B *Talk to him soothingly and try to persuade him to climb back in?* ◇

C *Phone the fire brigade?* ◇

―――――――――Question Four―――――――――

A KEY SUBORDINATE RESIGNS AFTER MISSING A PROMOTION. FINDING A REPLACEMENT COULD BE A LONG AND EXPENSIVE PROCESS. WOULD YOU:

A *Make him a handsome counter-offer?* ◇

B *Appeal to his loyalty and try to persuade him to withdraw his resignation?* ◇

C *Accept his resignation and immediately telephone a reputable firm of recruitment consultants?* ◇

Question Five

YOU HAVE TRAVELLED BY TRAIN TO ADDRESS AN IMPORTANT CONFERENCE. HAVING ARRIVED AT YOUR DESTINATION, YOU ARE LEAVING THE STATION WHEN YOU SUDDENLY REALISE THAT YOU HAVE LEFT YOUR BRIEFCASE ON THE TRAIN—WHICH HAS NOW DEPARTED. INSIDE THE BRIEFCASE ARE THE NOTES FOR YOUR SPEECH. YOU ARE DUE TO SPEAK IN AN HOUR'S TIME. WOULD YOU:

A *Phone the conference organiser and ask him to re-schedule your speech for later in the programme in order to give you more time to prepare?* ◇

B *Buy some postcards and write down the main headings of your talk in large capitals on cards?* ◇

C *Do nothing and decide to play it by ear?* ◇

Question Six

A SUBORDINATE BECOMES HIGHLY EMOTIONAL DURING A DISCUSSION ON HIS PERFORMANCE. YOU BEGIN TO FEAR THAT HE MAY ATTACK YOU. WOULD YOU:

A *Phone for help from the Security staff?* ◇

B *Assure him that you understand how he feels and are prepared to listen for as long as he wants to talk?* ◇

C *Assume a cheerful manner and suggest that you adjourn to the local pub to continue your discussions?* ◇

Question Seven

YOU ARE CHATTING TO A CUSTOMER IN YOUR OFFICE WHEN HE SUDDENLY COLLAPSES WITH A HEART ATTACK. HAVING CHECKED THAT HIS HEART IS STILL BEATING AND SENT FOR HELP, WOULD YOU:

A *Give him immediate mouth-to-mouth resuscitation?* ◇

B *Massage his heart?* ◇

C *Lay him on the floor, unbutton his shirt at the neck and loosen his tie and trouser belt?* ◇

Question Eight

44 BECAUSE OF A 'RUSH JOB', YOUR BOSS ASKS YOU

TO CANCEL A HALF-DAY'S HOLIDAY DURING WHICH YOU HAD PLANNED TO ATTEND THE PRIZE-GIVING AT YOUR SON'S SCHOOL, AT WHICH HE IS DUE TO RECEIVE A PRIZE. WOULD YOU:

A *Reluctantly agree and tell your son that you'll make it up to him later?* ◇

B *Ask your boss to reconsider, pointing out that your son has been looking forward for weeks to you being there?* ◇

C *Offer to come back to the office straight after the ceremony and to work until the job is done?* ◇

———————————Question Nine———————————

A SUBORDINATE TURNS DOWN AN OUTSTANDING PROMOTION OPPORTUNITY BECAUSE HIS OR HER PARTNER REFUSES TO RELOCATE. WOULD YOU:

A *Express your regrets and offer the job to someone else?* ◇

B *Invite the subordinate and his partner to discuss the matter with you over dinner at a smart restaurant?* ◇

C *Tell your subordinate that his partner's refusal could seriously damage his career?* ◇

———————————Question Ten———————————

YOU ARE HURTLING DOWN THE MOTORWAY, ALREADY LATE FOR A VITAL MEETING WITH A MAJOR CUSTOMER. SUDDENLY YOU SKID ON A PATCH OF ICE. WOULD YOU:

A *Jam on your brakes?* ◇

B *Turn into the skid?* ◇

C *Turn in the opposite direction to which you skid?* ◇

ARE YOU CO-OPERATIVE?

———————————NINETEEN———————————

However individualistic his nature, no executive can function entirely alone—he needs the co-operation of others to achieve his objectives. Increasingly, modern business is a complex network of interlocking functions and specialisations where those who need help must be ready to give it. Co-operation, like communication, is a two-way street.

The following questions will help to show you how co-operative you are:

Question One

YOU ARE JUST ABOUT TO LEAVE THE OFFICE TO GO HOME WHEN A COLLEAGUE REQUESTS YOUR HELP IN DEALING WITH A 'PANIC'. WOULD YOU:

A *Agree at once?* ◇

B *Try to persuade him that it can wait until tomorrow?* ◇

C *Refuse, saying that your partner is ill?* ◇

Question Two

A COLLEAGUE ASKS YOU TO MEET A VIP WHO IS ARRIVING ON A LATE-NIGHT FLIGHT, THEREBY ENABLING HIM TO VISIT HIS WIFE WHO IS IN HOSPITAL. WOULD YOU:

A *Agree at once?* ◇

B *Try to persuade him to find someone else?* ◇

C *Refuse, saying that you are having trouble with your car?* ◇

Question Three

A COLLEAGUE ASKS YOU TO GIVE HIS SON SOME ADVICE ON HIS CAREER (THE SON IS THINKING OF ENTERING THE SAME PROFESSION AS YOURSELF). WOULD YOU:

A *Agree at once?* ◇

B *Agree, but say that your information may be out of date and that he ought to read the latest book on the subject?* ◇

C *Agree, but say that you will only be able to spare him a few minutes?* ◇

Question Four

FOLLOWING YOUR EXCELLENT PRESENTATION AT A CONFERENCE, SEVERAL COLLEAGUES ASK YOU FOR COPIES OF THE TRANSPARENCIES WHICH YOU USED. WOULD YOU:

A *Agree—and act quickly to meet their requests?* ◇

B *Agree—but regard it as a very low priority?* ◇

C *Agree—and promptly forget about it?* ◇

———————Question Five———————

YOU RETURN FROM A TRAINING COURSE WITH
KNOWLEDGE OF A NEW TECHNIQUE WHICH
COULD BENEFIT A NUMBER OF YOUR
COLLEAGUES. WOULD YOU:

A *Talk to them about it and give them copies of the course handouts?* ◇

B *Discuss the course— but only in general terms?* ◇

C *Brush off all enquiries, saying that the course was a waste of time?* ◇

———————Question Six———————

A LOCAL HEADMASTER ASKS IF YOU WILL GIVE
AN EVENING TALK ABOUT YOUR COMPANY TO A
GROUP OF SCHOOL LEAVERS. THE DATE
COINCIDES WITH THE FINAL EPISODE OF YOUR
FAVOURITE TV SERIAL. WOULD YOU:

A *Agree at once?* ◇

B *Agree—but try to persuade him to change the date?* ◇

C *Refuse—pleading a previous engagement?* ◇

———————Question Seven———————

A MAJOR CUSTOMER OF ONE OF YOUR
COLLEAGUES TELEPHONES, REQUESTING THE
URGENT REPLACEMENT OF A DEFECTIVE PART. IT
IS 5.30 PM ON A FRIDAY. YOUR COLLEAGUE HAS
GONE ON HOLIDAY AND THE SERVICE ENGINEER
HAS GONE HOME. THE CUSTOMER'S PREMISES ARE
30 MILES FROM YOUR OFFICE. WOULD YOU:

A *Jump in your car and deliver the part personally?* ◇

B *Phone the service engineer and tell him to deal with it right away?* ◇

C *Tell the customer that nothing can be done until after the weekend?* ◇

———————Question Eight———————

A COLLEAGUE WHO IS ALSO YOUR CLOSEST

47

RIVAL FOR PROMOTION ASKS IF HE CAN BORROW A BEST-SELLING MANAGEMENT BOOK WHICH HE HAS SEEN YOU READING. WOULD YOU:

A *Agree at once?* ◇

B *Agree—but tell him it was useless?* ◇

C *Tell him that you left it on a train?* ◇

Question Nine

A COLLEAGUE ASKS YOU TO ALTER YOUR SUMMER HOLIDAY DATES SO THAT HE CAN OBTAIN A RESERVATION WHICH IS ONLY AVAILABLE DURING THE TWO WEEKS YOU HAVE CHOSEN. YOU HAVE NOT YET BOOKED YOUR OWN HOLIDAY. WOULD YOU:

A *Agree at once?* ◇

B *Tell him that you'll discuss it with your wife?* ◇

C *Refuse—telling him that you have already booked?* ◇

Question Ten

YOU ARE DRIVING HOME—ALREADY LATE FOR AN EVENING ENGAGEMENT—WHEN YOU SEE YOUR SECRETARY STANDING AT THE SIDE OF THE ROAD, LOOKING HELPLESSLY AT A PUNCTURED TYRE ON HER CAR. WOULD YOU:

A *Pull in immediately and change the tyre for her?* ◇

B *Tell her that you can't stop but that you'll ask a garage to send someone to help her?* ◇

C *Drive past, pretending that you haven't seen her?* ◇

DO YOU HAVE A POSITIVE ATTITUDE?

TWENTY

There are periods in every executive's career when nothing seems to go right—when plans are overturned, ideas rejected and budgets melt away like snow-flakes in the sun. These are the times when he wonders 'Is it worth it?' and thinks perhaps of changing his job. But if and when he does so he finds that nothing has changed: every job, however challenging, has its ups and downs.

How do you react to adversity? Can you think and act positively even when things are at their worst?

Question One

YOU HAVE JUST GIVEN A PRESENTATION AT A MAJOR COMPANY CONFERENCE WHICH HAS BEEN POORLY RECEIVED—MAINLY DUE TO YOUR LACK OF SPEAKING SKILLS. WOULD YOU:

A *Accept it philosophically and hope for a better reception next time?* ◇

B *Resolve to prepare more carefully in future?* ◇

C *Enrol immediately for a course in public speaking?* ◇

Question Two

A MAJOR CUSTOMER HAS WRITTEN TO THE CHAIRMAN, COMPLAINING BITTERLY ABOUT THE POOR QUALITY OF THE LAST CONSIGNMENT OF PRODUCT AND OF THE GENERAL INEFFICIENCY OF THE AFTER-SALES SERVICE. YOU ARE THE SALES MANAGER. WOULD YOU:

A *Write to the customer, promising a full investigation?* ◇

B *Replace the faulty consignment immediately and make an urgent appointment with the customer to discuss ways of improving the after-sales service?* ◇

C *Instruct a representative to call to pacify the customer?* ◇

Question Three

YOU HAVE WORKED EXTREMELY HARD TO FINISH A RUSH JOB ON TIME. YOUR BOSS, WHO HAD GIVEN YOU THE ASSIGNMENT, RECEIVES YOUR REPORT WITHOUT A WORD OF THANKS. WOULD YOU:

A *Show by your manner how strongly you resented it?* ◇

B *Console yourself with the thought that you had met a tough challenge?* ◇

C *Complain bitterly to your colleagues about your boss's behaviour?* ◇

---Question Four---

DURING A HEATED DISCUSSION AT A MEETING, ONE OF YOUR COLLEAGUES IS EXTREMELY RUDE TO YOU. WOULD YOU:

A *Hit back furiously in similar fashion?* ◇

B *Ignore the personal attack and calmly re-state your point of view?* ◇

C *Remain silent, hoping that someone will spring to your defence?* ◇

---Question Five---

YOUR NEWLY-APPOINTED BOSS SEEMS A MUCH COLDER AND LESS APPROACHABLE PERSON THAN THE PREVIOUS HIGHLY CONVIVIAL ONE. WOULD YOU:

A *Let everyone know how uncomfortable he makes you feel?* ◇

B *Keep out of his way as much as possible?* ◇

C *Suspend judgment until you get to know him better?* ◇

---Question Six---

YOU HAVE BEEN STUDYING PART-TIME FOR A PROFESSIONAL QUALIFICATION. YOU HAVE JUST RECEIVED NEWS THAT YOU HAVE FAILED TO PASS THE FINAL EXAMINATION. WOULD YOU:

A *Find out when you could re-sit the exam?* ◇

B *Decide to call it a day and concentrate upon your job?* ◇

C *Decide to do nothing immediately but to re-assess the situation in three months' time?* ◇

---Question Seven---

YOU ARE OFFERED A SIGNIFICANT PROMOTION— BUT IT WILL MEAN MOVING TO AN UNATTRACTIVE PART OF THE COUNTRY. WOULD YOU:

A *Accept and determine to make the best of it?* ◇

B *Turn it down, saying that you wouldn't be happy living there?* ◇

C *Push for an extra-large salary increase to compensate you for loss of 'quality of life'?* ◇

—————————Question Eight—————————

YOU HAVE ACCUSED ONE OF YOUR SUBORDINATES OF MAKING A SERIOUS ERROR. EVIDENCE EMERGES WHICH PROVES THAT YOU WERE WRONG. WOULD YOU:

A *Call him into your office and apologise?* ◇

B *Not apologise but go out of your way to treat him more kindly in future?* ◇

C *Tell one of his friends that you now know what really happened?* ◇

—————————Question Nine—————————

ONE OF YOUR CLOSEST FRIENDS AT THE OFFICE HAS TAKEN A DECISION WHICH HAS MADE HIM VERY UNPOPULAR IN THE COMPANY (YOU TOO DISAPPROVE). WOULD YOU:

A *Try to avoid being seen in his company?* ◇

B *Remain friendly and helpful in your personal relations?* ◇

C *Make it clear to him that your friendship is over?* ◇

—————————Question Ten—————————

YOU ARRIVE HOME TO FIND THAT YOUR WIFE HAS LEFT YOU. THE NEXT DAY YOU ARE DUE TO SIGN A MULTI-MILLION POUND CONTRACT WITH A MAJOR CUSTOMER. WOULD YOU:

A *Go ahead and sign the contract?* ◇

B *Telephone the customer and request that the meeting be postponed for a few days?* ◇

C *Get a subordinate to handle the contract while you deal with your domestic affairs?* ◇

—————————Question Eleven—————————

YOU ARE INVOLVED IN A MOTORING ACCIDENT WHICH RESULTS IN YOUR HAVING TO STAY IN HOSPITAL FOR SEVERAL WEEKS. AS YOU BEGIN TO RECOVER, HOW WOULD YOU SPEND YOUR TIME? WOULD YOU:

A Mostly watch T.V. and listen to the radio? ◇

B Catch up on all those classic novels you'd always wanted to read? ◇

C Arrange to deal with some of your office paperwork and for your subordinates to visit you to keep you informed? ◇

―――――――――――――Question Twelve―――――――――

YOU DISCOVER THAT YOUR SECRETARY (WHO IS OFF SICK) HAS FAILED TO PREPARE SOME HANDOUTS FOR AN IMPORTANT MEETING WHICH YOU ARE DUE TO ATTEND IN TEN MINUTES' TIME. WOULD YOU:

A Phone the chairman of the meeting and request that your presentation be held over until the next meeting? ◇

B Adapt your presentation so as to minimise the lack of handouts and explain to the group that they will be receiving them later? ◇

C Try to persuade the chairman to amend the agenda so that your presentation becomes the final item—hoping that by then the group will be tired and less critical? ◇

ARE YOU A WORKAHOLIC?

test

―――――――――――TWENTY-ONE――――――――――

Hard work and long hours are familiar companions for most executives: there is no place in business for the easily-fatigued. However, the work-obsessed executive is not always the most effective performer. Indeed, by failing to broaden his interests and to take proper recreation, he may easily become dull and jaded and even damage his health.

Are you in danger of becoming a workaholic? The following test will tell you.

1. Do you ever work before breakfast?

Frequently ◇   Very rarely ◇   Never ◇

2. Are you usually the first to arrive at the office?

Yes ◇   Occasionally ◇   No ◇

3. Do you work through your lunch break?

Frequently ◇   Occasionally ◇   Never ◇

4. Are you usually the last to leave the office?

Yes ◇   Occasionally ◇   No ◇

5. Do you work at home during the evening?

Frequently ◇   Sometimes ◇   Never ◇

6. Do you telephone your staff during the evening or at weekends to discuss work problems?

Frequently ◇   Sometimes ◇   Never ◇

7. Do you lie awake at night thinking about work problems?

Frequently ◇   Occasionally ◇   Never ◇

8. Do you ever get up during the night and begin working?

Sometimes ◇   Very rarely ◇   Never ◇

9. Do you take work home at weekends?

Frequently ◇   Sometimes ◇   Never ◇

10. Do you ever come into the office on Saturdays or Sundays?

Often ◇   Occasionally ◇   Never ◇

11. Do you take your full annual holiday entitlement?

Never ◇   Usually ◇   Always ◇

12. Have you ever cancelled a holiday because of work?

Sometimes ◇   Very rarely ◇   Never ◇

13. Have you ever cancelled a family outing or anniversary celebration because of work pressure?

Sometimes ◇   Very rarely ◇   Never ◇

14. Do you take work with you on holiday?

Frequently ◇   Occasionally ◇   Never ◇

15. Do you ever contact the office while you are on holiday?

Frequently ◇   Occasionally ◇   Never ◇

16. Do you read material unrelated to work in your spare time?

Very rarely ◇   Frequently ◇   Always ◇

17. Are you reluctant to delegate, preferring to do the important jobs yourself?

Yes ◇   Sometimes ◇   No ◇

18. Have your ever refused to attend training programmes because of pressure of work?

Often ◇   Occasionally ◇   Never ◇

19. Have you ever been advised by a doctor to take things easier?

Often ◇   Occasionally ◇   Never ◇

20. Have members of your family ever complained about the hours you work?

Frequently ◇   Occasionally ◇   Never ◇

CAN YOU MANAGE YOUR TIME?

TEST TWENTY-TWO

Time is the scarcest resource. It can never be replaced, there is never as much of it as you need and, not least, it costs money. An organisation will succeed or fail depending upon how effectively its employees use their time.

Managing time means, first of all, managing oneself. The following test will help you to measure how well you are doing—answer each question YES or NO (*tick for yes, cross for no*).

DO YOU:

1. Make a list of priority tasks as soon as you arrive at work?   ◇

2. Try to complete one job at a time, instead of flitting from task to task?   ◇

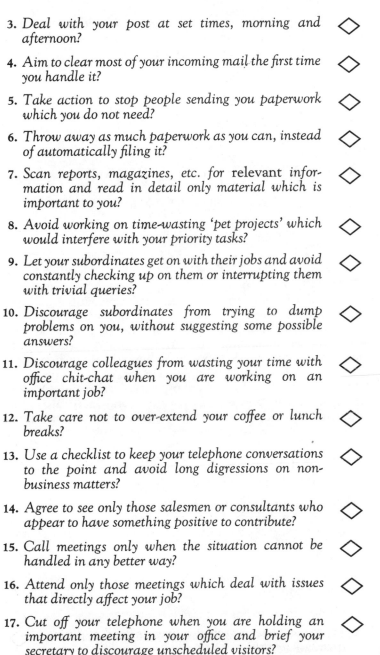

3. Deal with your post at set times, morning and afternoon?

4. Aim to clear most of your incoming mail the first time you handle it?

5. Take action to stop people sending you paperwork which you do not need?

6. Throw away as much paperwork as you can, instead of automatically filing it?

7. Scan reports, magazines, etc. for relevant information and read in detail only material which is important to you?

8. Avoid working on time-wasting 'pet projects' which would interfere with your priority tasks?

9. Let your subordinates get on with their jobs and avoid constantly checking up on them or interrupting them with trivial queries?

10. Discourage subordinates from trying to dump problems on you, without suggesting some possible answers?

11. Discourage colleagues from wasting your time with office chit-chat when you are working on an important job?

12. Take care not to over-extend your coffee or lunch breaks?

13. Use a checklist to keep your telephone conversations to the point and avoid long digressions on non-business matters?

14. Agree to see only those salesmen or consultants who appear to have something positive to contribute?

15. Call meetings only when the situation cannot be handled in any better way?

16. Attend only those meetings which deal with issues that directly affect your job?

17. Cut off your telephone when you are holding an important meeting in your office and brief your secretary to discourage unscheduled visitors?

18. *Seek help when dealing with problems which require specialist expertise or experience, instead of wasting time trying to solve them single-handed?* ◇

19. **Make full use of time-saving equipment such as computers and copying machines?** ◇

20. **Before leaving the office, make a note of any tasks not yet completed for inclusion on the next day's action list?** ◇

HOW COMPETITIVE ARE YOU?

test

────────TWENTY-THREE────────

The higher you go in management, the fewer the opportunities for further advancement—and the greater the competition when jobs fall vacant. As you rise and rise in the organisation, the pyramid narrows towards its apex and you find yourself struggling to maintain a foothold upon what has suddenly become a very slippery ladder.

Are you cut out for the competitive struggle? Do you blossom or wilt when the heat is on? Here are some questions to test your mettle—answer each question Yes or No (*tick for yes, cross for no*):

1. *Do you have the stamina for sustained hard work?* ◇

2. *Are you always on the look-out for new ideas?* ◇

3. *Are you constantly trying to improve your performance?* ◇

4. *Do you insist upon high standards for yourself and others?* ◇

5. *Do you seize opportunities to improve your operation?* ◇

6. *Do you enjoy selling your ideas to other people?* ◇

7. *Can you cope with setbacks without becoming discouraged?* ◇

8. Do you enjoy tackling problems which people tell you are 'insoluble'? ◇

9. Can you take tough decisions which may make you unpopular? ◇

10. Do you relish the challenge of meeting tight deadlines? ◇

11. Do you enjoy working under continuous pressure? ◇

12. Do you believe that an executive should 'lead from the front'? ◇

13. Can you analyse complex problems and identify the key issues? ◇

14. Can you cope with the stress of high-risk decision-making? ◇

15. Are you skilled at anticipating the consequences of your decisions? ◇

16. Are you stimulated by the competition of high-calibre rivals? ◇

17. Do you have a network of useful contacts throughout the organisation? ◇

18. Are you a good listener? ◇

19. Do you get along with most people, including your boss? ◇

20. Do you take every opportunity to publicise the work of your group? ◇

21. Do you write occasional articles for the company newspaper? ◇

22. Are you a good public speaker? ◇

23. Are you prepared to undertake outside assignments (e.g. speaking at conferences, getting involved in community activities, etc.) which help to project a favourable image of the organisation? ◇

24. Are you quick to assess the implications of changes in corporate structure and/or promotions in other parts of the organisation? ◇

25. Have you trained someone in your group who could take over from you if you were promoted? ◇

26. *Do you have a regular reading schedule which keeps you abreast of new developments in your field?* ◇

27. *Do you ever volunteer your group when the company is seeking an opportunity to try out new methods and techniques?* ◇

28. *Can you be forceful without antagonising others?* ◇

29. *Have you discussed your ambitions with your boss— and won his support?* ◇

30. *Do you positively enjoy competition and conflict?* ◇

DO YOU TRUST PEOPLE?

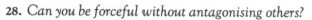

———————TWENTY-FOUR———————

An executive is responsible not only for his own performance: he is equally accountable for the performance of his team. But good teamwork is virtually impossible without a high level of trust between the members of the team—and between the team and the executive who leads them.

Whether you trust people largely depends upon your view of human nature. Do this test and discover how trusting you really are.

——————————*Question One*——————————

YOU ARE ABOUT TO GO ON HOLIDAY AND HAVE SEVERAL MAJOR PROJECTS AWAITING COMPLETION. BEFORE YOUR DEPARTURE DO YOU:

A *Brief your subordinates about what action to take while you are away and delegate the necessary authority to enable them to make decisions?* ◇

B *Ask them to collect any further information which you may require and have it ready for your return?* ◇

C *Instruct them to leave everything until you return?* ◇

——————————*Question Two*——————————

YOU RETURN FROM HOLIDAY TO FIND A NUMBER OF EXPENSE CLAIMS AWAITING AUTHORISATION.

UNLESS YOU SIGN THEM TODAY THE CLAIMANTS
WILL HAVE TO WAIT AN EXTRA MONTH FOR
PAYMENT. YOU ALSO HAVE A SUBSTANTIAL
BACKLOG OF CORRESPONDENCE TO DEAL WITH.
WOULD YOU:

A *Check only those exceeding a certain figure?* ◇

B *Check each one meticulously?* ◇

C *Sign all of them without checking them?* ◇

―――――――――――Question Three――――――――――――

YOU ARE INVITED TO COMPLETE A
QUESTIONNAIRE AS PART OF A COMPANY-
SPONSORED ATTITUDE SURVEY. MANY OF THE
QUESTIONS PERMIT STRONG CRITICISMS TO BE
MADE OF COMPANY POLICY. YOU ARE ASSURED
THAT YOUR REPLIES WILL BE TREATED AS
STRICTLY CONFIDENTIAL. WOULD YOU:

A *Give favourable responses to all questions, even if* ◇
they are not always true?

B *Make some critical comments―but only on relatively* ◇
minor issues?

C *Complete the questionnaire with total honesty?* ◇

――――――――――――Question Four――――――――――――

YOU ARE INFORMED IN CONFIDENCE THAT A
SUBORDINATE IS BEING CONSIDERED FOR AN
OVERSEAS POSTING. OUTSIDE THE OFFICE YOU
ARE VERY FRIENDLY WITH THE INDIVIDUAL
CONCERNED. WOULD YOU:

A *Tell him in confidence that he is being considered?* ◇

B *Engineer an informal discussion with him about his* ◇
career aspirations and hint vaguely about 'overseas
possibilities'?

C *Do nothing and let events take their course?* ◇

――――――――――――Question Five――――――――――――

YOUR BOSS SAYS THAT HE WOULD LIKE TO GET
TO KNOW YOUR SUBORDINATES BETTER AND
PROPOSES TO MEET THEM INDIVIDUALLY ONCE A
MONTH IN HIS OFFICE. WOULD YOU:

A *Agree at once and set up a timetable for the meetings?* ◇

B *Oppose the proposal, fearing that it would undermine your authority?* ◇

C *Agree—but on condition that you sit in?* ◇

—————————————Question Six—————————————

A COLLEAGUE WITH WHOM YOU HAVE HAD A RATHER DISTANT RELATIONSHIP BECOMES MUCH MORE FRIENDLY AND BEGINS TO CULTIVATE YOU. WOULD YOU:

A *Remain on guard until you found out what he wanted?* ◇

B *Respond in a friendly manner but let him make all the running?* ◇

C *Respond warmly to his approaches and treat him virtually as a long-lost friend?* ◇

—————————————Question Seven—————————————

YOUR COMPANY ENGAGES A CONSULTANT TO INVESTIGATE CERTAIN MANAGEMENT POLICIES. HE REQUESTS AN INTERVIEW WITH YOU. DO YOU:

A *Answer his questions succinctly, neither misleading him nor volunteering information?* ◇

B *Respond with caution, making no criticisms of current practices?* ◇

C *Participate enthusiastically and tell him everything you know?* ◇

—————————————Question Eight—————————————

YOU AND A COLLEAGUE FROM ANOTHER DEPARTMENT ARE ATTENDING A SEMINAR RUN BY AN OUTSIDE TRAINING ORGANISATION. THE LECTURER INVITES EACH PARTICIPANT TO SAY WHAT HE REALLY THINKS ABOUT HIS BOSS. WOULD YOU:

A *Respond with complete objectivity, mentioning both good and bad points?* ◇

B *Mention only your boss's good points, in case any criticism should get back to him after the course?* ◇

C *Make some criticisms—but not the ones that you feel most strongly about?* ◇

ARE YOU A GOOD INTERVIEWER?

---TWENTY-FIVE---

Being able to pick good people is one of the executive's most important skills—one which can make all the difference between managing a high-performance group and one with poor productivity and low morale. Whether you are interviewing internal or external candidates, you need a *systematic approach*, not one which is based upon prejudice and guesswork.

Imagine that you are about to interview an experienced external candidate for a key supervisory position in your group. This test will show you how effective you are:

---*Question One*---

WHAT DO YOU CONSIDER THE MOST IMPORTANT PREREQUISITE FOR A SUCCESSFUL SELECTION INTERVIEW, I.E. ONE WHICH RESULTS IN THE APPOINTMENT OF THE RIGHT CANDIDATE?

A *A clear and up-to-date job specification?* ◇

B *A comfortable interviewing room?* ◇

C *A friendly interviewer?* ◇

---*Question Two*---

HAVING READ ALL THE AVAILABLE INFORMATION ABOUT THE CANDIDATE (C.V., APPLICATION FORM, ETC.), WOULD YOU:

A *Prepare some questions relating to his experience?* ◇

B *Prepare a few 'trick questions' which have always seemed to work well in the past?* ◇

C *Play it by ear—ask whatever questions seem to be most appropriate at the time?* ◇

---*Question Three*---

YOU HAVE WELCOMED THE CANDIDATE, ARRANGED FOR COFFEE AND CUT OFF YOUR TELEPHONE. HOW WOULD YOU BEGIN THE INTERVIEW? WOULD YOU:

A *Try to relax him by chatting about the weather?* ◇

B *Ask him about one of his hobbies or interests?* ◇

C *Enquire what kind of journey he had?* ◇

Question Four
HAVING PUT HIM AT EASE, WHAT WOULD BE YOUR NEXT STEP? WOULD YOU:

A *Ask him to tell you about himself?* ◇

B *Question him in detail about his most recent work experience?* ◇

C *Ask him about his educational qualifications?* ◇

Question Five
SINCE THE JOB INVOLVES SUPERVISING SEVERAL PEOPLE, YOU WOULD LIKE TO KNOW WHAT THE CANDIDATE THINKS ABOUT A NUMBER OF 'PEOPLE MANAGEMENT' ISSUES. WOULD YOU:

A *Ask him questions in such a way that only a 'yes' or 'no' answer is required?* ◇

B *Give him your own views and ask him to comment?* ◇

C *Ask him open-ended questions, using phrases such as 'how do you feel about' or 'how would you approach'?* ◇

Question Six
THE CANDIDATE EXPRESSES AN OPINION ON AN IMPORTANT ISSUE WITH WHICH YOU STRONGLY DISAGREE. WOULD YOU:

A *Tell him so in no uncertain terms?* ◇

B *Stay silent or pose a supplementary question?* ◇

C *Terminate the interview immediately?* ◇

Question Seven
THE CANDIDATE ASKS YOU A QUESTION ABOUT CAREER PROSPECTS. HOW WOULD YOU HANDLE IT? WOULD YOU:

A *Tell him that 'the sky's the limit'?* ◇

B *Outline the company's career development policy and discuss some possible career paths?* ◇

C *Murmur that 'It's a little too early to be thinking about these things—it's best to concentrate on doing your current job'?* ◇

Question Eight

HAVING COMPLETED YOUR QUESTIONING OF THE CANDIDATE, WHAT WOULD BE YOUR FINAL STEP? WOULD YOU:

A *Thank him for attending and wish him a safe journey home?* ◇

B *Invite him to ask some further questions or to volunteer any additional information which had not emerged during the interview?* ◇

C *Ask him if he would accept the job if it were offered to him?* ◇

Question Nine

WHEN INTERVIEWING SEVERAL CANDIDATES, IT IS UNWISE FOR AN INTERVIEWER TO RELY WHOLLY UPON HIS MEMORY. HOW WOULD YOU RESOLVE THIS PROBLEM? WOULD YOU:

A *Use a tape recorder?* ◇

B *Make your own brief notes during the interview?* ◇

C *Ask a colleague or a subordinate to sit in on the interview?* ◇

Question Ten

HOW MUCH TALKING DO YOU BELIEVE THE INTERVIEWER HIMSELF SHOULD DO? SHOULD HE:

A *Simply ask his prepared questions and note the replies?* ◇

B *Talk for at least half of the time in order to impress the candidate with his knowledge and experience—thus hoping to attract an ambitious person who is keen to learn?* ◇

C *Let the candidate do the bulk of the talking but keep him well supplied with questions, both prepared and spontaneous?* ◇

ARE YOU A GOOD AMBASSADOR FOR YOUR COMPANY?

---TWENTY-SIX---

From time to time every executive finds himself called upon to represent his company in the outside world. For some these contacts may be mainly with customers, for others it may mean attending conferences or meetings. Whatever the occasion, it is important that he makes a good impression. He is, in effect, his company's ambassador.

Do you see such contacts as a threat or as an opportunity? Here are some questions to help you evaluate your performance.

---Question One---

IF YOU RECEIVED AN INVITATION TO SPEAK AT AN OUTSIDE MEETING ON A TOPIC WITH WHICH YOU WERE COMPLETELY FAMILIAR, WOULD YOU:

A *Nearly always accept?* ◇

B *Sometimes accept?* ◇

C *Nearly always refuse?* ◇

---Question Two---

IF YOU WERE INVITED TO SPEAK ON A TOPIC WHICH WOULD INVOLVE YOU IN SUBSTANTIAL PREPARATION, WOULD YOU:

A *Nearly always accept?* ◇

B *Sometimes accept?* ◇

C *Decline the invitation?* ◇

---Question Three---

EVEN THOUGH THE TOPIC DID NOT REQUIRE YOU TO TALK ABOUT YOUR COMPANY'S PRODUCTS AND SERVICES, WOULD YOU:

64 **A** *Make a few discreet references to them?* ◇

B *Spend a good deal of time talking about them?* ◇

C *Not refer to them at all?* ◇

─────────────Question Four─────────────

IF YOU WERE INVITED TO WRITE AN ARTICLE FOR
A MANAGEMENT, PROFESSIONAL OR TRADE
MAGAZINE, WOULD YOU:

A *Nearly always accept?* ◇

B *Sometimes accept?* ◇

C *Nearly always refuse?* ◇

─────────────Question Five─────────────

IF YOUR SPEECH OR ARTICLE RESULTED IN A
NUMBER OF LETTERS FROM PEOPLE SEEKING
YOUR ADVICE, WOULD YOU:

A *Deal with them personally?* ◇

B *Delegate the replies to a subordinate?* ◇

C *Ignore them?* ◇

─────────────Question Six─────────────

IF YOU WERE ASKED A QUESTION DURING A
PRESENTATION, THE ANSWER TO WHICH YOU
PROMISED TO SEND THE QUESTIONER AFTER THE
MEETING, WOULD YOU:

A *Find out the answer and write back or telephone as* ◇
quickly as possible?

B *Deal with it as and when you could find the time?* ◇

C *Do nothing—hoping the questioner had forgotten* ◇
your promise?

─────────────Question Seven─────────────

AFTER YOU HAD GIVEN A PRESENTATION AT A
CONFERENCE, WOULD YOU SEND A SHORT
'THANK YOU' NOTE TO THE CHAIRMAN AND/OR
THE PERSON WHO HAD LOOKED AFTER YOU AT
THE CONFERENCE?

A *Always.* ◇

B *Sometimes.* ◇

C *No.* ◇ 65

Question Eight

IF YOU WERE APPROACHED BY A LOCAL
HEADMASTER REQUESTING YOU TO ARRANGE A
TOUR OF YOUR FACTORY OR OFFICES FOR A
GROUP OF SIXTH-FORM PUPILS, WOULD YOU:

A *Nearly always accept?* ◇

B *Sometimes accept?* ◇

C *Nearly always refuse?* ◇

Question Nine

A BUSINESS SCHOOL STUDENT WRITES TO YOU
ASKING WHETHER HE COULD INTERVIEW YOU IN
CONNECTION WITH A THESIS WHICH HE IS
WRITING. WOULD YOU:

A *Nearly always accept?* ◇

B *Sometimes accept?* ◇

C *Nearly always refuse?* ◇

Question Ten

YOUR PROFESSIONAL ASSOCIATION REQUESTS
YOUR CO-OPERATION IN A MEMBERSHIP SURVEY
WHICH WOULD REQUIRE YOU TO COMPLETE A
VOLUMINOUS QUESTIONNAIRE. WOULD YOU:

A *Complete and return it quickly?* ◇

B *Complete it only if and when you received a reminder?* ◇

C *Ignore it?* ◇

CAN YOU HANDLE CONSULTANTS?

test

---TWENTY-SEVEN---

There are many circumstances in which any executive,
no matter how competent, finds that he needs outside
help. Management consultants exist to provide such help
and yet sometimes the cure can be worse than the disease.
It all depends upon whether you, the patient, can select the

right doctor and whether his skills are relevant to your particular problem. The important thing is to work *with* your consultant, not abdicate responsibility and simply hope for the best.

Using consultants can be an expensive process. Suppose that you had a serious problem in your group—how would you ensure that you received value for money?

—Question One—
FOR WHICH OF THE FOLLOWING REASONS WOULD YOU CALL IN CONSULTANTS?

A *The problem requires special skills which are not available in the organisation.*

B *You feel that you need objective advice.*

C *You can't think of anything else to do.*

—Question Two—
HOW WOULD YOU SET ABOUT CHOOSING A CONSULTANT? WOULD YOU:

A *Contact a well-known firm you had read about in the press?*

B *Get recommendations from business contacts with recent relevant experience of consultants?*

C *Choose from a list of reputable consultants supplied by a professional management association?*

—Question Three—
HAVING IDENTIFIED SOME POSSIBLE CANDIDATES FOR THE ASSIGNMENT, HOW WOULD YOU CHECK OUT EACH FIRM'S TRACK RECORD? WOULD YOU:

A *Telephone or visit your business contacts who had used them?*

B *Write to your contacts, enclosing a list of questions?*

C *Ask each consultancy to supply client references?*

—Question Four—
BEFORE MEETING A CONSULTANT FOR AN EXPLORATORY INTERVIEW, WOULD YOU:

A *Try to familiarise yourself with some of the concepts and jargon that he would be likely to use?*

67

B *Rely upon him to explain things to you?*

C *Get some of your contacts to brief you?*

Question Five

ASSUME THAT YOU HAVE SELECTED YOUR
CONSULTANT, WORKED WITH HIM TO DEFINE THE
PROBLEM AND ACCEPTED HIS ACTION PLAN (AND
FEE). WOULD YOU NOW:

A *Tell him to get on with it and keep you posted?*

B *Specify by when and in what form you expect him to submit his final report?*

C *Arrange to meet him for regular progress reviews?*

Question Six

IF THE CONSULTANT WITH WHOM YOU HAD BEEN
NEGOTIATING WAS NOT THE ONE WHO WOULD
BE CARRYING OUT THE ASSIGNMENT, WOULD
YOU:

A *Specify the qualifications and personality of the person you wanted and interview the individual recommended by his firm?*

B *Leave it to the senior consultant to select an appropriate individual?*

C *Consult some of your contacts with experience of consultants and seek their advice on the type of person to look for?*

Question Seven

BEFORE THE PROJECT BEGINS, THOSE MEMBERS OF
YOUR STAFF WHO WILL BE WORKING WITH THE
CONSULTANT WILL NEED TO BE BRIEFED. WOULD
YOU:

A *Leave it to the consultant to handle?*

B *Put out a briefing note to the individuals involved?*

C *Give each individual a personal briefing?*

Question Eight

AS THE ASSIGNMENT PROGRESSES, HOW WOULD
YOU DEAL WITH THE CURIOSITY (AND, PERHAPS,
APPREHENSION) OF THE STAFF WHO ARE
INVOLVED? WOULD YOU:

A Call them together for regular informal feedback sessions which you would run yourself? ◇

B Request the consultant to report back at such meetings? ◇

C Assure everyone that they will be briefed on the consultant's final recommendations and given an opportunity to air their views? ◇

———————Question Nine———————

IF IT SHOULD TRANSPIRE THAT THE CONSULTANT WAS BEHAVING IN A HIGH-HANDED MANNER AND UPSETTING KEY MEMBERS OF YOUR STAFF, WOULD YOU:

A Request his superiors to replace him with another experienced consultant with a more congenial personality? ◇

B Discuss the situation with both the consultant and the individuals concerned and try to iron out the difficulties? ◇

C Tell your staff that they will have to 'grin and bear it' until the project is completed? ◇

———————Question Ten———————

ASSUMING THAT YOU HAVE ACCEPTED THE CONSULTANT'S FINAL REPORT, WOULD YOU:

A Ensure that before leaving he trained members of your staff to help you to implement his recommendations? ◇

B Request his assistance in implementing at least the first phase of the follow-up strategy? ◇

C Implement the recommendations yourself, using whatever personnel were currently available and without bothering about any special training? ◇

CAN YOU SELL YOUR IDEAS?

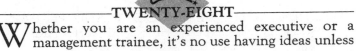

———————TWENTY-EIGHT———————

Whether you are an experienced executive or a management trainee, it's no use having ideas unless **69** you can put them across. The ability to present a convincing case is a key executive skill—one which can be as relevant to accountants and engineers as it is to salesmen and copywriters.

Suppose that you are scheduled to present a proposal for approval to a senior management meeting in your company. How would you cope with the following situations?

————————————Question One————————————

BEFORE BEGINNING THE DETAILED PLANNING OF YOUR PRESENTATION, YOU WOULD DO WELL TO CONSIDER CERTAIN BACKGROUND FACTORS. WHICH OF THE FOLLOWING WOULD YOU CONSIDER MOST IMPORTANT?

A *The time at which your presentation is scheduled?*

B *The size and shape of the room in which the meeting will be held?*

C *The likely attitudes of those attending towards your proposal?*

————————————Question Two————————————

YOU HAVE BEEN CALLED UPON TO PRESENT YOUR PROPOSAL. HOW WOULD YOU BEGIN? DO YOU:

A *Tell a humorous story which you recently heard on television?*

B *State your proposal briefly and outline how you plan to present it?*

C *Assure the audience that your idea is not as complicated as it may seem?*

————————————Question Three————————————

BEFORE EXPLAINING YOUR PROPOSAL IN DETAIL, ON WHICH OF THE FOLLOWING ISSUES WOULD YOU FEEL IT PRUDENT TO SPEND SOME TIME?

A *A detailed breakdown of the costs involved?*

B *The weaknesses and shortcomings of the present situation—and why remedial action is urgently required?*

C *The additional resources needed to implement the proposal?*

Question Four
WHEN EXPLAINING YOUR PROPOSAL, WOULD YOU:

A *Give most weight to the technical aspects?*

B *Stress the advantages—and provide back-up data wherever possible?*

C *Emphasise that it is a brand-new approach?*

Question Five
WHEN DEALING WITH DETAILED COSTS OR COMPLEX TECHNICAL DATA, WOULD YOU:

A *Read out the figures from a prepared sheet?*

B *Use clear visual aids?*

C *Distribute a handout containing the figures?*

Question Six
JUST AS YOU ARE ABOUT TO COVER A KEY SECTION OF YOUR PRESENTATION, A SECRETARY ENTERS WITH A MESSAGE FOR SOMEONE IN THE GROUP. WOULD YOU:

A *Carry on speaking as if nothing had happened?*

B *Stop—but visibly fume with annoyance?*

C *Say 'Shall we just pause for a moment to give Mr. X a chance to deal with this? I'm sure he won't be long'?*

Question Seven
YOU HAVE ONE MINUTE LEFT. HOW WOULD YOU END YOUR PRESENTATION? WOULD YOU:

A *Make an emotional appeal for the audience's support?*

B *Remind them briefly of the advantages and end with a powerful punch-line?*

C *Say that you hope that they will support your proposal and thank them for giving you so much of their time?*

Question Eight
DURING THE QUESTION PERIOD AFTER YOUR PRESENTATION, ONE QUESTIONER HAS CLEARLY MISSED ONE OF YOUR MOST IMPORTANT POINTS. WOULD YOU:

71

A *Wait for him to finish and then repeat the point, showing how it meets his particular concern?* ◇

B *Interrupt him, pointing out that you covered the point during your presentation but that you are willing to go over it again?* ◇

C *Apologise for not having communicated properly the first time?* ◇

Question Nine

A MEMBER OF THE GROUP, SENIOR IN STATUS TO YOU, ATTACKS YOUR PROPOSAL VIGOROUSLY. HOW WOULD YOU RESPOND? WOULD YOU:

A *Back-pedal instantly, admitting that you could be wrong?* ◇

B *Remain calm and try to identify some areas of agreement?* ◇

C *Counter-attack forcefully and try to demolish his arguments?* ◇

Question Ten

EVEN THE MOST IMPRESSIVE PROPOSALS OFTEN HAVE SOME DISADVANTAGES. HOW WOULD YOU DEAL WITH THEM? WOULD YOU:

A *Point them out straightforwardly but emphasise the much greater advantages?* ◇

B *Only deal with them if someone mentions them?* ◇

C *Mention them but dismiss them as being of little account?* ◇

DO YOU TAKE CARE OF YOUR HEALTH?

test

TWENTY-NINE

In the cut-and-thrust of competitive business, an executive must be physically as well as mentally fit. Yet for many executives life is a seemingly endless round of business lunches, customer entertainment and stressful journeys by plane or car. In time even the strongest constitution may be affected and the executive's career seriously undermined.

What kind of shape are you in? Are you looking after your health or simply hoping for the best?

1. *Do you smoke?*

    a *Heavily* ◇   **b** *Hardly ever* ◇   **c** *Not at all* ◇

2. *Do you take exercise?*

    a *Daily* ◇   **b** *Weekly* ◇   **c** *Not at all* ◇

3. *How often do you go for a 30-minute walk?*

    a *Daily* ◇   **b** *Weekly* ◇   **c** *Never* ◇

4. *Are you overweight?*

    a *Substantially* ◇   **b** *Slightly* ◇   **c** *Not at all* ◇

5. *How many inches of fat can you pinch around your middle?*

    a *Less than an inch* ◇   **b** *About an inch* ◇

    c *More than an inch* ◇

6. *Can you fit into clothes which you bought two years ago?*

    a *Easily* ◇   **b** *With difficulty* ◇   **c** *No chance* ◇

7. *Can you touch your toes?*

    a *Easily* ◇   **b** *Only as far as my ankles* ◇

    c *Only as far as my knees* ◇

8. *Do you get breathless walking upstairs?*

    a *Frequently* ◇   **b** *Occasionally* ◇   **c** *Never* ◇

9. *If you had to run 50 yards to catch a bus, how breathless would you be?*

    a *Very breathless* ◇   **b** *Somewhat breathless* ◇

    c *Not at all breathless* ◇

10. *Do you experience pains in your chest?*

    a *Frequently* ◇   **b** *Occasionally* ◇   **c** *Never* ◇

11. *Do you drink alcohol?*

    a *Heavily* ◇   **b** *Moderately* ◇   **c** *Occasionally* ◇

12. *Do you eat sweets and rich, fatty foods?*

    a *Frequently* ◇   **b** *Sometimes* ◇   **c** *Rarely* ◇

13. *Do you eat fresh fruit and vegetables?*

    a *Frequently* ◇   **b** *Sometimes* ◇   **c** *Rarely* ◇

14. *Do you take sugar?*

    a *More than 10 spoonfuls daily* ◇

    b *Less than 10 spoonfuls daily* ◇   **c** *None* ◇

15. *Do you find it difficult to relax?*

    a *Frequently* ◇   **b** *Sometimes* ◇   **c** *Never* ◇

16. *Do you lose your temper easily?*

    a *Frequently* ◇   **b** *Sometimes* ◇   **c** *Never* ◇

17. *Do you find it difficult to get to sleep at night?*

    a *Frequently* ◇   **b** *Sometimes* ◇   **c** *Never* ◇

18. *Do you lie awake at night worrying about your problems?*

    a *Frequently* ◇   **b** *Sometimes* ◇   **c** *Never* ◇

19. *Do you take any kind of drug to calm you down?*

    a *Frequently* ◇   **b** *Sometimes* ◇   **c** *Never* ◇

20. *How often do you have a complete medical check-up?*

    a *Annually* ◇   **b** *Every 2–3 years* ◇   **c** *Never* ◇

CAN YOU TAKE TOUGH DECISIONS?

test

THIRTY

It is not difficult to give praise and receive applause but to give and take criticism is far more demanding. Often an executive must deal with highly sensitive situations which require tact and discretion if trouble is to be avoided. Nevertheless, there are times when nettles must be grasped and a more direct approach is entirely appropriate. Like most other aspects of decision-making it is a question of *judgment*.

How would you handle the following situations?

--------Question One--------

IF YOU WERE AT A MEETING AND WERE TOTALLY IGNORANT OF THE TOPIC BEING DISCUSSED, WOULD YOU:

A *Stay quiet and wait for the next subject?*

B *Ask the chairman to give you a quick briefing so that you were able to follow the discussion?*

C *Ask one or two questions to show interest?*

--------Question Two--------

IF ONE OF YOUR MOST TALENTED SUBORDINATES STARTED COMING IN LATE FOR WORK, DO YOU:

A *Admonish him to be more punctual in the interests of good discipline?*

B *Try to find out the reason for his lateness and make your decision after hearing his explanation?*

C *Turn a blind eye so as to avoid a possible confrontation?*

--------Question Three--------

IF YOUR BOSS ORDERED YOU TO CARRY OUT A TASK WHICH YOU FELT WAS UNNECESSARY, WOULD YOU:

A *Comply with the order because he was the boss?*

B *Try to persuade him to change his mind?*

C *Tell him that you would do it—but under protest?*

--------Question Four--------

SUPPOSE THAT YOU WERE REVIEWING A SUBORDINATE'S PERFORMANCE WHEN SUDDENLY HE BEGAN TO CRITICISE YOUR MANAGEMENT STYLE. WOULD YOU:

A *Listen carefully and encourage him to be completely frank?*

B *Cut him short but promise to discuss his criticisms on another occasion?*

C *Reject his criticisms and counter-attack vigorously?* ◇

―――――――――――Question Five―――――――――――
YOU HEAR ON THE GRAPEVINE THAT ONE OF
YOUR COLLEAGUES HAS BEEN SPREADING A FALSE
RUMOUR ABOUT YOU. WOULD YOU:

A *Ignore the individual concerned but determine to have* ◇
your revenge?

B *Discuss the matter with him to establish whether your* ◇
grapevine information was correct?

C *Confront him and express your anger in no uncertain* ◇
terms?

―――――――――――Question Six―――――――――――
YOU SENSE THAT A COLLEAGUE WHO USED TO BE
FRIENDLY IS NOW TRYING TO AVOID YOU.
WOULD YOU:

A *Drop into his office and try to find out what is wrong?* ◇

B *Do nothing, hoping that it is just a passing phase?* ◇

C *Begin avoiding him too?* ◇

―――――――――――Question Seven―――――――――――
IF YOU WERE TO MISS A PROMOTION ON WHICH
YOU HAD SET YOUR HEART, WOULD YOU:

A *Express your disappointment to your boss and ask for* ◇
an explanation?

B *Accept it philosophically and hope for better luck next* ◇
time?

C *Start looking for a job outside the company?* ◇

―――――――――――Question Eight―――――――――――
IF YOU DELEGATED A COMPLEX TASK TO A
SUBORDINATE WHICH YOU SUSPECTED HE
WOULD DISLIKE DOING, WOULD YOU:

A *Leave it to him to decide whether to complain to you?* ◇

B *Tell him why you had chosen him and how he would* ◇
benefit from the additional experience?

C *Use flattery to try to win him over?* ◇

―――――――――――Question Nine―――――――――――
IF ONE OF YOUR COLLEAGUES MADE A

PRESENTATION TO AN IMPORTANT CUSTOMER
WHICH YOU FELT CONTAINED SOME NOTABLE
SHORTCOMINGS, WOULD YOU:

A *Say nothing unless he asked you for your comments—* ◇
and then assure him that it was 'O.K.'?

B *Point out some of the more important weaknesses and* ◇
suggest how they might be remedied in future?

C *Suggest that he should attend a public speaking* ◇
course?

———————————Question Ten———————————
YOU GIVE YOUR SECRETARY A LAST-MINUTE
RUSH ASSIGNMENT WHICH WILL NECESSITATE
HER WORKING LATE. SHE ASKS 'WHY THE PANIC?'
AND IS CLEARLY ANNOYED. WOULD YOU:

A *Tell her that you haven't got time to explain now but* ◇
that you'll tell her in the morning?

B *Point out that you hardly ever ask her to stay on after* ◇
normal hours and that she ought not to complain
about the occasional late duty?

C *Explain why the job is so urgent and express your* ◇
appreciation for her efforts?

———————————Question Eleven———————————
YOU ARE TRYING TO PLACATE AN ANGRY
CUSTOMER ON THE TELEPHONE WHEN THE
CHAIRMAN DROPS IN FOR A CHAT. WOULD YOU:

A *Tell the customer that you'll ring him back?* ◇

B *Continue the conversation in the chairman's* ◇
presence?

C *Break off for a moment to explain the situation to the* ◇
chairman and ask him if you can telephone him as
soon as you have finished?

———————————Question Twelve———————————
A SUBORDINATE EXPRESSES A STRONG INTEREST
IN A PROMOTION VACANCY IN ANOTHER
DEPARTMENT AND ASKS YOU TO RECOMMEND
HIM. YOU FEEL THAT HE IS NOT SUFFICIENTLY
QUALIFIED FOR THE JOB. WOULD YOU: 77

A *Remain non-committal, saying that you'll have to think it over?* ◇

B *Give him the impression that you'll be supporting him—but in fact do nothing?* ◇

C *Explain why you feel you can't recommend him on this occasion but discuss what action he might take to strengthen his chances for future vacancies—and offer to help him?* ◇

DO YOU CARE ABOUT PEOPLE?

Test

---THIRTY-ONE---

People aren't just pawns to be pushed around on the boss's chessboard: they are individuals with opinions and values of their own. To lead them effectively, an executive must show that he is sensitive to their needs and use persuasion rather than authority to win their co-operation. For while it is rare for staff to rebel openly, it is not difficult for them to sabotage an unpopular boss.

Pawns or people? Robots or individuals? This test will show whether you really care about your staff—answer Yes or No (*tick for yes, cross for no*).

1. *Are you sincerely interested in the people who report to you?* ◇

2. *Do you have a rigid set of rules by which you tend to judge other people?* ◇

3. *Do you see people as 'types' rather than as complex individuals?* ◇

4. *Can you tolerate your subordinates disagreeing with you without becoming angry or resentful?* ◇

5. *Can you accept ways of doing a job which may be different from your own?* ◇

6. When dealing with people who are emotionally upset, are you able to remain objective while understanding how they feel? ◇

7. If an argument develops among your subordinates, are you quick to take sides? ◇

8. Can you deal with unpleasant situations without becoming unpleasant yourself? ◇

9. When you are in a discussion, are you usually impatient for the other person to finish so that you can make your point? ◇

10. Do you find it difficult to keep another person's confidences? ◇

11. Can you communicate criticism in a constructive manner? ◇

12. Do you usually react immediately to any situation which annoys you, even if the issue is relatively minor? ◇

13. Do you encourage your subordinates to discuss their feelings towards you and the way you manage them? ◇

14. If the feedback is critical, do you become upset? ◇

15. Do you provide candid feedback to your subordinates about your feelings towards them? ◇

16. Do you take the initiative in dealing with troubled employees? ◇

17. Do you believe that a boss should train and develop his staff? ◇

18. Do you consult your subordinates and allow them to participate in decision-making? ◇

19. Do you encourage them to put forward new ideas? ◇

20. Do you believe that it is possible to change the attitudes people have towards their work? ◇

21. Do you believe that it is generally unwise to be open and trusting in relationships at work? ◇

22. Can you tolerate unorthodox individuals in your team? ◇

23. *Do you believe that material factors are the most powerful motivators?* ◇

24. *Do you believe that most people will avoid working whenever they get the chance?* ◇

25. *Do you enjoy building an effective working group?* ◇

26. *Do you take pride in the successes of members of your team?* ◇

27. *Do you bring their achievements to the attention of your boss?* ◇

28. *Do you create opportunities for your subordinates to meet higher management?* ◇

29. *Would you allow a subordinate to chair a meeting at which you were present?* ◇

30. *Do you encourage your subordinates to develop themselves?* ◇

HOW GOOD A POLITICIAN ARE YOU?

test

THIRTY-TWO

Many of the most important things about business are never taught in the business schools. True, you can acquire knowledge and learn techniques but this is barely the tip of the managerial iceberg. Beneath the surface are those *political* skills which no one talks about— but which can sometimes make the difference between success and failure.

How skilled are you at dealing with political situations?

Question One

YOUR BOSS COMES UP WITH AN IDEA FOR A NEW PRODUCT WHICH YOU BELIEVE WILL BE A DISASTER. WOULD YOU:

80 A *Try to persuade him to drop the idea?*

B *Suggest that he should commission a market research report ('just to be on the safe side')?* ◇

C *Stay quiet and hope for the best?* ◇

———————————Question Two———————————
YOU SUSPECT (BUT HAVE NO CONCLUSIVE
EVIDENCE) THAT ONE OF YOUR AREA MANAGERS
IS FIDDLING HIS EXPENSES. WOULD YOU:

A *Nominate him for the first suitable vacancy which occurs outside your department?* ◇

B *Assign him to a head office job where you can keep an eye on him?* ◇

C *Request the Internal Audit department to carry out an in-depth investigation into his expense claims?* ◇

———————————Question Three———————————
YOUR BOSS'S PARTNER MAKES A PASS AT YOU AT
THE CHRISTMAS DANCE. WOULD YOU:

A *Respond enthusiastically?* ◇

B *Change the subject?* ◇

C *Suggest that they both join you and your partner for a drink at the bar?* ◇

———————————Question Four———————————
YOU ARE OFFERED PROMOTION TO A POSITION
WHICH IS LOCATED 200 MILES FROM HEAD OFFICE
AND ARE WORRIED ABOUT BEING OVERLOOKED
WHEN FUTURE OPPORTUNITIES OCCUR. WOULD
YOU:

A *Insist that you are re-assigned to head office within a definite period?* ◇

B *Turn the job down?* ◇

C *Accept and send frequent reports back to head office, with copies to the executives you are anxious to impress?* ◇

———————————Question Five———————————
YOUR BOSS MAKES YOU THE BUTT OF SOME
RATHER HEAVY-HANDED WIT AT A COMPANY
SOCIAL FUNCTION. WOULD YOU:

A *Hit back with a joke or story at his expense?* ◇ 81

B *Show what a good sport you are by laughing loudest of all?* ◇

C *Remain silent and stony-faced?* ◇

---Question Six---

A HIGHLY-TALENTED SUBORDINATE WISHES TO HIRE SOMEONE ABOUT WHOM YOU HAVE STRONG RESERVATIONS. WOULD YOU:

A *Let him go ahead in the interests of harmony?* ◇

B *Suggest that he obtains an independent assessment from a psychologist or consultant?* ◇

C *Refuse to accept his recommendation?* ◇

---Question Seven---

YOUR BOSS REBUKES YOU FOR A MISTAKE WHICH YOU HAVE MADE. WOULD YOU:

A *Apologise and thank him for his helpful criticism?* ◇

B *Argue that the error was not all that serious?* ◇

C *Try to apportion some of the blame to other people?* ◇

---Question Eight---

A SUBORDINATE IS STRONGLY OPPOSED TO YOUR PLANS FOR RE-ORGANISING YOUR DEPARTMENT. YOUR ATTEMPTS TO PERSUADE HIM TO CHANGE HIS MIND HAVE FAILED. WOULD YOU:

A *Threaten to fire him unless he co-operates?* ◇

B *Promise him a more important job in the new organisation if he withdraws his opposition?* ◇

C *Obtain your boss's approval to send him away for a month on a management course and re-organise your group during his absence?* ◇

---Question Nine---

A POWER STRUGGLE DEVELOPS BETWEEN TWO GROUPS OF EXECUTIVES, EACH OF WHICH IS ANXIOUS TO GAIN YOUR SUPPORT. WOULD YOU:

A *Throw in your lot with whichever faction seemed most likely to win?* ◇

82 B *Remain strictly neutral?* ◇

C *Appear to be sympathetic to both points of view, without committing yourself to either?* ◇

---Question Ten---

AFTER THE CHAIRMAN RETURNS FROM A BUSINESS SCHOOL COURSE, HE ORDERS A NEW MANAGEMENT SYSTEM TO BE IMPLEMENTED THROUGHOUT THE COMPANY. YOU BELIEVE IT TO BE BOTH UNSOUND AND UNNECESSARY. WOULD YOU:

A *Seek an interview with him and implore him to reconsider?* ◇

B *Express 100% support and throw yourself into implementing the system?* ◇

C *Obey the chairman's instructions but not over-zealously, not wishing to be discredited if and when the system fails?* ◇

---Question Eleven---

YOUR BOSS STEALS ONE OF YOUR BEST IDEAS AND PASSES IT OFF AS HIS OWN. WOULD YOU:

A *Demand that he acknowledges that it was your idea?* ◇

B *Complain bitterly to your colleagues and murmur about resigning?* ◇

C *Accept the situation but let it be known discreetly where the credit really lies?* ◇

---Question Twelve---

YOUR BOSS IS SITTING UPON A REPORT WHICH, IF IMPLEMENTED, COULD RESULT IN MAJOR COST SAVINGS FOR THE ORGANISATION. WOULD YOU:

A *Keep badgering him for his comments?* ◇

B *Send a copy of your report to your boss's boss?* ◇

C *Try to obtain the support of someone close to top management to act as 'a friend at court'?* ◇

DO YOU COMMUNICATE EFFECTIVELY?

THIRTY-THREE

Communication is the work an executive does to secure *understanding* between himself and others. It is a vital skill, the catalyst that transforms ideas into action. Without it an executive is like a shipwrecked sailor, waiting to be sighted by a passing ship; with it he is like the master of that ship who knows where he is going and how to get there.

Which are you: the shipwrecked sailor or the master of the ship?—answer Yes or No (*tick for yes, cross for no*).

1. *Do you hold regular meetings of your group, not only to discuss work issues but also to communicate matters of general interest?*   ◇

2. *Do you actively encourage questions and discussion?*   ◇

3. *Do you follow up these meetings with a list of action points, designating the persons responsible for taking action, together with target dates for completion of each assignment?*   ◇

4. *Do you hold regular meetings with each of your subordinates to review progress against objectives— objectives which you have discussed and agreed with the individual concerned?*   ◇

5. *Does each of your subordinates have a copy of his objectives?*   ◇

6. *Are you approachable—do you encourage your subordinates to communicate with you informally?*   ◇

7. *Do you occasionally hold meetings of your group outside the office (e.g. in a hotel) in order to encourage informal communication in a relaxed atmosphere?*   ◇

8. *Does each of your subordinates have a job description, outlining his key responsibilities?*   ◇

9. *Is each of your subordinates clear about the limits of his authority?*

10. *Do you formally appraise the performance of each of your subordinates at least once a year and discuss their appraisals with them, encouraging them to speak frankly about any problems or concerns?*

11. *Do you encourage each individual to discuss his ambitions and help him to plan his next career step?*

12. *Are you a good listener?*

13. *Do you keep your boss well briefed about the progress of the work and the performance of your people?*

14. *Do you encourage your subordinates to communicate and co-operate with each other?*

15. *Have you ever formed a task force or a committee within your group, not only as a means of solving a problem but also to encourage them to work together?*

16. *Where appropriate, do you discuss your problems with your subordinates and invite their comments and suggestions?*

17. *Do you encourage your people to seek help and advice, where appropriate, from other specialist groups—and likewise to co-operate when their own advice is sought?*

18. *When there is a major reorganisation within the company, or an important change in policy or working practice, do you call your people together and explain the reasons for the change and how it will affect them?*

19. *Do you give your people as much advance notice as possible of such changes?*

20. *Do you have a company/departmental policy manual which your subordinates can consult (assuming that they do not have their own copies)?*

21. *When your boss holds meetings, do you keep your colleagues informed of developments in your area which could affect their work?*

22. *Do you communicate promptly to your subordinates*

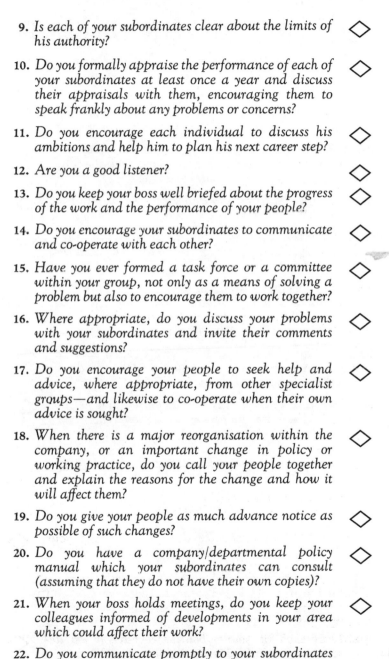

85

any decisions taken at such meetings which either will or could affect their work? ◇

23. Do you run occasional brainstorming sessions with your people to encourage them to put forward new ideas? ◇

24. Wherever possible, do you communicate with your people on a face-to-face basis rather than in writing? ◇

25. In your written communications, do you make only sparing use of terms such as 'confidential'—and encourage your subordinates to do the same? ◇

26. Do you write as clearly and succinctly as possible, avoiding jargon and 'officialese'? ◇

27. Do you take particular care to avoid jargon when speaking or writing to people who are not specialists in your field? ◇

28. If the company were to engage consultants to undertake a major project, would you call your people to a meeting to explain the purpose of the project and how it would affect them? ◇

29. If you heard that your staff were worried about a rumour which you knew to be unfounded, would you hold a meeting to set the record straight? ◇

30. When a subordinate has done an outstanding job, do you congratulate him personally as soon as possible? ◇

HOW AMBITIOUS ARE YOU?

THIRTY-FOUR

Ambition is as natural to an executive as flight is to a bird but that doesn't mean that every executive's dreams come true. Inevitably, perhaps, the majority are disappointed—some because their goals were pitched higher than their abilities, others because they sat back and hoped for the best.

Yet while no one can foretell what the future holds, the shrewd executive tries to 'make things happen' and to establish himself as a promotion contender long before a vacancy occurs.

Are you actively *preparing yourself* for promotion or simply trusting to luck? Answer Yes or No (*tick for yes, cross for no*). Have you:

1. *Identified your short-term promotion goal—the job which you hope to be doing in, say, three to four years' time?* ◇

2. *Identified what additional knowledge, skill and experience you will need in order to be a realistic candidate?* ◇

3. *Analysed your performance in your current job and identified those areas where you need to improve?* ◇

4. *Discussed your aspirations with your boss and/or the company personnel executive and sought their advice on what action to take?* ◇

5. *Checked on the career paths of other people who have held the job in which you are interested, including the current occupant?* ◇

6. *Discussed your ambitions with business friends and contacts outside the company whose judgment you respect?* ◇

7. *Drawn up a realistic action plan for achieving your goal?* ◇

8. *Applied to attend management training courses in subjects which are relevant to your career plan?* ◇

9. *Encouraged your boss to give you projects which will help to fill the gaps in your experience?* ◇

10. *Investigated whether there are any evening classes available locally which could help you?* ◇

11. *Considered taking a correspondence course to obtain a relevant qualification?* ◇

12. *Sought the advice of the company personnel/training executive regarding some books and journals which you ought to read?* ◇

13. Consider joining the local branch of your professional association to keep up-to-date and to enlarge your circle of business contacts? ◇

14. Considered writing for any company publications which could bring you to the attention of higher management? ◇

15. Established some review dates at which you will check your progress towards achieving your goal? ◇

HOW WELL-READ ARE YOU?

test

————————THIRTY-FIVE————————

Reading management books will not, of itself, make you a better manager but to refuse to read at all is to risk becoming obsolete. Like any other professional— doctor, lawyer, architect—the effective executive reads both to keep his knowledge up to date and to harvest new ideas.

Are you reading as widely as you should?

————————*Question One*————————
HOW MANY MANAGEMENT BOOKS DO YOU READ ON AVERAGE DURING A YEAR?

A *More than 4.* ◇

B *Less than 4.* ◇

C *None.* ◇

————————*Question Two*————————
HOW MANY BUSINESS JOURNALS DO YOU READ EACH MONTH?

A *More than 4.* ◇

B *Less than 4.* ◇

88 C *None.* ◇

Question Three
HOW OFTEN DO YOU READ THE BUSINESS PAGES OF YOUR NEWSPAPERS?

A *Daily.* ◇

B *Frequently.* ◇

C *Never.* ◇

Question Four
THE PRACTICE OF MANAGEMENT IS WIDELY REGARDED AS ONE OF THE MOST INFLUENTIAL BUSINESS BOOKS OF THE TWENTIETH CENTURY. WHO WROTE IT?

A *Peter Drucker.* ◇

B *Alfred P. Sloan.* ◇

C *Warren Bennis.* ◇

Question Five
WHICH MANAGEMENT BOOK TOPPED THE U.S. BEST-SELLER LISTS FOR SEVERAL MONTHS IN 1984?

A The One Minute Manager *by Spencer Johnson & Kenneth Blanchard.* ◇

B In Search of Excellence *by Thomas J. Peters & Robert H. Waterman.* ◇

C Further Up the Organisation *by Robert Townsend.* ◇

Question Six
I'M O.K.—YOU'RE O.K. BY THOMAS HARRIS AND GAMES PEOPLE PLAY BY ERIC BERNE ARE RECOMMENDED READING FOR EXECUTIVES INTERESTED IN:

A *Keep-fit programmes?* ◇

B *Transactional analysis?* ◇

C *Psychological testing?* ◇

Question Seven
WHICH U.S. UNIVERSITY PRODUCES THE WORLD'S MOST PRESTIGIOUS MANAGEMENT JOURNAL?

A *Princeton.* ◇

B *Yale.* ◇ 89

C *Harvard.* ◇

Question Eight

WHICH BRITISH BUSINESS ACADEMIC IS
GENERALLY REGARDED AS THE FATHER OF
'ACTION LEARNING' (SEE HIS BOOK *DEVELOPING
EFFECTIVE MANAGERS*)?

A *Prof. Charles Handy.* ◇

B *Prof. John Adair.* ◇

C *Prof. Reg Revans.* ◇

Question Nine

THE FAMOUS 'THEORY X—THEORY Y' ANALYSIS
OF MANAGEMENT STYLES WAS FIRST PRESENTED
IN WHICH NOTABLE BOOK?

A The Human Side of Enterprise *by Douglas McGregor.* ◇

B The Effective Executive *by Peter Drucker.* ◇

C Parkinson's Law *by C. Northcote Parkinson.* ◇

Question Ten

WHICH U.S. BUSINESS JOURNAL IS FAMOUS FOR
PUBLISHING ITS ANNUAL 'LEAGUE TABLE' OF THE
TOP 500 AMERICAN CORPORATIONS?

A The Wall Street Journal. ◇

B Fortune. ◇

C Business Week. ◇

ARE YOU LEADING A BALANCED LIFE?

test

---THIRTY-SIX---

All work and no play makes Jack (or Jill) a dull executive. The difference between enjoying one's work and being obsessed by it is often the difference
between success and failure since even the most reliable

batteries occasionally need re-charging. To neglect family, friends and other interests is a certain recipe for 'executive burn-out'—that saddest of stages when a manager's energies suddenly desert him, leaving him a shadow of his former self.

Are you keeping your life in balance—answer Yes or No (tick for yes, cross for no)?

1. Do you have a hobby which involves you in making things? ◇

2. Do you have a hobby which involves you in collecting things? ◇

3. Do you have an artistic hobby (painting, writing, sculpting, etc.)? ◇

4. Do you actively participate in any sport or game? ◇

5. Do you regularly attend sporting events? ◇

6. Do you read at least one fiction or non-fiction book per month? ◇

7. Do you attend at least three concerts a year (classical, rock or jazz)? ◇

8. Do you go to the theatre at least three times a year? ◇

9. Do you visit art galleries or exhibitions? ◇

10. Are you a member of your local amateur dramatic society? ◇

11. Are you a member of any social club? ◇

12. Do you enjoy attending parties? ◇

13. Do you give at least three dinner or cocktail parties each year? ◇

14. Do you enjoy eating in smart restaurants? ◇

15. Do you have a wide circle of friends outside the office? ◇

16. Do you work for any charitable cause? ◇

17. Do you work for any social cause (conservation of the environment, etc.)? ◇

18. Are you an active member of a political party? ◇

19. *Are you involved in local church affairs?* ◇

20. *Are you involved in youth work, including Scouts, Guides, etc.?* ◇

21. *Do you attend the meetings of your Parent-Teacher Association?* ◇

22. *Do you enjoy do-it-yourself activities in conjunction with your home or car?* ◇

23. *Are you a keen gardener?* ◇

24. *Are you a hi-fi enthusiast?* ◇

25. *Do you keep or breed animals?* ◇

26. *Do you enjoy motoring for pleasure at weekends?* ◇

27. *Do you enjoy travelling abroad?* ◇

28. *Are you learning a foreign language?* ◇

29. *Are you studying some other non-business subject?* ◇

30. *Do you take a close interest in current affairs?* ◇

HOW TOLERANT ARE YOU?

test

THIRTY-SEVEN

In the hurly-burly of management there is a time to fight and a time to retreat, a time to assert yourself and a time to be patient. There will be many moments too when you must recognise that people have every right to hold opinions with which you may strongly disagree or to behave in ways which may run counter to your beliefs. In short, without in any way giving up your own opinions, values and standards, you must learn to be tolerant.

This test will help to show you how tolerant you are.

YOU RECEIVE A NUMBER OF COMPLAINTS ABOUT YOUR DEPARTMENT, SOME FROM COLLEAGUES, OTHERS FROM CUSTOMERS. HOW WOULD YOU REACT? WOULD YOU REGARD THEM AS:

A *A nuisance—and almost certainly unjustified?* ◇

B *A personal attack upon your efficiency?* ◇

C *An opportunity to improve the quality of your product or service?* ◇

A COLLEAGUE, WHO WAS FORMERLY A SUBORDINATE, WINS A PROMOTION ON WHICH YOU HAD SET YOUR HEART. WOULD YOU:

A *Appear to accept the situation—but secretly start looking for another job?* ◇

B *Congratulate him or her?* ◇

C *Complain to everyone that you had been robbed of a job which was rightfully yours?* ◇

YOU ARE ATTENDING A MANAGEMENT TRAINING COURSE. DURING THE OPENING FEW MINUTES THE SPEAKER MAKES A COMMENT WITH WHICH YOU STRONGLY DISAGREE. WOULD YOU:

A *Immediately and forcefully voice your objection?* ◇

B *Conclude that the speaker is a fool—and stop listening?* ◇

C *Make a note of your point and ask a question at the first opportune moment?* ◇

YOU ARE INTERVIEWING FOR A VACANCY IN YOUR GROUP AND THE BEST-QUALIFIED CANDIDATE'S ONLY DRAWBACK—IN YOUR EYES— IS HIS HAIR STYLE AND MODE OF DRESS. WHAT EFFECT WOULD THIS HAVE UPON YOUR DECISION? WOULD YOU:

A *Reject his application on some other pretext?* ◇

B *Offer him the job regardless?* ◇ 93

C *Offer him the job but resolve to have a word with him after he has joined?* ◇

Question Five

YOU FIND OUT THAT A MEMBER OF YOUR STAFF IS HAVING A HOMOSEXUAL RELATIONSHIP. HOW WOULD YOU REACT? WOULD YOU:

A *Make sure that the person concerned knew of your disapproval?* ◇

B *Do nothing—believing that an individual's sexual preferences are his own affairs?* ◇

C *Do nothing—but delete his name from your list of promotable people?* ◇

Question Six

A POLICY WHICH YOU INTRODUCED SEVERAL YEARS AGO COMES UNDER ATTACK FROM A BRIGHT YOUNG SUBORDINATE. WOULD YOU:

A *Listen carefully and comment only when you are sure that you have understood his criticisms?* ◇

B *Vigorously reject his arguments half-way through his explanation, pointing out his youthful inexperience of such weighty matters?* ◇

C *Agree to investigate his ideas—and promptly forget about them?* ◇

Question Seven

IF YOUR ORGANISATION WERE TO ANNOUNCE THAT IT INTENDED TO MAKE A SUBSTANTIAL DONATION TO A MAJOR CULTURAL PROJECT, WOULD YOU:

A *Regard it as a highly public-spirited act?* ◇

B *Denounce it as a waste of shareholders' money?* ◇

C *Dismiss it as a cynical piece of public relations?* ◇

Question Eight

A LONG-SERVING SUBORDINATE GETS DRUNK AT AN OFFICE PARTY AND MAKES A REMARK WHICH YOU FIND OFFENSIVE. WOULD YOU:

94 A *Express your anger and tell him to go home?* ◇

B *Ignore the remark—but determine to have it out with him the next time you are in the office?* ◇

C *Say nothing—but resolve to mention it at his appraisal interview in three months' time?* ◇

―――――――――――――*Question Nine*―――――――――――――
YOUR SECRETARY TURNS UP AN HOUR LATE FOR WORK ON A MORNING WHEN SHE WAS DUE TO TAKE THE MINUTES AT AN IMPORTANT MEETING. WOULD YOU:

A *Ask her to take her place at the meeting and take the matter up with her later on?* ◇

B *Tell her that there's no point in her staying now that the meeting is nearly over—and send her back to the office?* ◇

C *Appear to accept her apology—but make a note to see the Personnel Manager about getting her replaced?* ◇

―――――――――――――*Question Ten*―――――――――――――
YOU SIT IN ON A LECTURE BEING GIVEN BY A SUBORDINATE TO SOME IMPORTANT VISITORS. HE INCORRECTLY QUOTES SOME STATISTICS IN SUPPORT OF ONE OF HIS MAIN POINTS. WOULD YOU:

A *Correct him at once?* ◇

B *Point out his error to him in private during the coffee break?* ◇

C *Say nothing in case you might offend him?* ◇

CAN YOU WRITE CLEARLY?

test

―――――――――――――THIRTY-EIGHT―――――――――――――

The ability to write effectively is an essential executive skill. Busy managers have no time to sift through pages of verbiage in search of the one or two points that really **95** matter. They need to find what they are looking for quickly and easily and to understand clearly what is required of them.

Can you write clear letters, memos and reports—or do you only succeed in confusing your readers? Test yourself against the following questions—answer Yes or No (*tick for yes, cross for no*):

1. *Before you write to anyone, are you always clear about what you are trying to achieve, i.e. your objective or message?* ◇

2. *Do you consider your reader's requirements, i.e. how he is hoping to benefit from reading what you have written?* ◇

3. *Do you consider what your reader already knows about the subject?* ◇

4. *Do you know the purpose for which your letter, memo or report is likely to be used?* ◇

5. *Where you know your reader personally, do you take into account his temperament and personality, opinions and feelings?* ◇

6. *Before writing a complicated letter or report, do you prepare a framework or plan so that your writing is well-organised and logical?* ◇

7. *Do you tell your reader all that he needs to know in order to be able to understand your message?* ◇

8. *Do you exclude material which he does not need to know and which might confuse him?* ◇

9. *Do you always use a short, clear title or subject heading to focus the reader's attention?* ◇

10. *Do you get to the point as quickly as possible without lengthy and unnecessary preambles?* ◇

11. *Do you use short words, short sentences and short paragraphs?* ◇

12. *Do you avoid using 'buzz words' or jargon which your reader may not understand?* ◇

13. *Do you avoid using pompous phrases which could obscure your message and irritate your reader?* ◇

14. Are your paragraphs carefully linked to each other, avoiding too many different themes in the same paragraph?

15. Does your writing flow logically from one point to the next, avoiding constant backtracking to issues already covered?

16. Wherever possible, do you use active rather than passive verbs?

17 Do you use adjectives and adverbs sparingly so as to maximise their impact?

18. Do you use only as much punctuation as is necessary to make the meaning clear?

19. Do you write so that your reader can clearly distinguish between facts and opinions?

20. Do you try to 'sell' your ideas in terms of your reader's interests?

21. Is the tone of your letters friendly and helpful?

22. Wherever possible, do you address your letters to individuals rather than to organisations?

23. When giving instructions or requesting action, is the tone of your writing courteous and persuasive rather than domineering and autocratic?

24. Do you always check your letters for 'howlers' and spelling mistakes?

25. Do you ensure that your name and job title are typed beneath your signature?

26. When writing a report, do you group your material under clear, logical headings and sub-headings?

27. Are your facts complete, relevant and clear?

28. Do you ensure that your reader understands the significance of the facts which you present, i.e. what they mean for him?

29. Are your facts under the right headings?

30. Are your statements correct, with no unjustified exaggerations or avoidable inaccuracies?

31. *Do you support any generalisations with specific examples?* ◇

32. *Can your reader distinguish clearly between your conclusions and your recommendations?* ◇

33. *Do you use a simple, functional style, eschewing 'fine writing' or 'literary English'?* ◇

34. *Are any items adding to the clarity of your message, i.e. diagrams, sketches, graphs, tables, etc., all clear and self-explanatory?* ◇

DO YOU WELCOME A CHALLENGE?

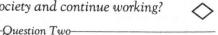

THIRTY-NINE

For today's executive life could scarcely be more exciting. New techniques, faster communications, tigerish competition—here are the challenges which separate the professionals from the amateurs, the doers from the talkers, the achievers from the dreamers.

In an unpredictable world the ability to respond to a challenge has never been more vital. How do *you* rate on this key success factor?

Question One

IF YOU WERE TO INHERIT A SUBSTANTIAL SUM OF MONEY, WOULD YOU:

A *Leave your secure job and start your own business?* ◇

B *Authorise a stockbroker to invest it in stocks and shares?* ◇

C *Put it into a building society and continue working?* ◇

Question Two

A VISITING SPEAKER FAILS TO TURN UP TO ADDRESS A SENIOR MANAGEMENT MEETING WHICH YOU HAVE ORGANISED. WOULD YOU:

98

A *Apologise for his absence and cancel the meeting?* ◇

B *Organise an impromptu discussion on a topic of general interest?* ◇

C *Show a management training film which you believe would benefit many of those present?* ◇

--------------------Question Three--------------------

COMPANY PROFITS ARE FALLING AND YOUR BOSS INSTRUCTS YOU TO ACHIEVE HIGHER PRODUCTIVITY ON A REDUCED BUDGET AND WITH FEWER PEOPLE. WOULD YOU:

A *Declare it to be impossible?* ◇

B *Launch a cost-cutting drive?* ◇

C *Call a meeting of your group, explain the situation and invite everyone present to contribute their ideas?* ◇

--------------------Question Four--------------------

YOU ARE INVITED TO PRESENT A PAPER AT THE PRESTIGIOUS NATIONAL CONFERENCE OF YOUR PROFESSIONAL ASSOCIATION. YOU DISLIKE PUBLIC SPEAKING AND FIND IT AN ORDEAL. WOULD YOU:

A *Accept—and begin working on your speech?* ◇

B *Decline on the grounds that you are a poor speaker?* ◇

C *Accept—and find out where you can get some training in public speaking?* ◇

--------------------Question Five--------------------

A CABARET ARTISTE AT A COMPANY SOCIAL FUNCTION ASKS YOU TO ASSIST HER WITH HER ACT. WOULD YOU:

A *Accept—after a fair amount of persuasion?* ◇

B *Decline, pleading that you are far too shy?* ◇

C *Leap on to the stage, although you are inwardly quaking with fright?* ◇

--------------------Question Six--------------------

YOUR BOSS IS TAKEN ILL HALF AN HOUR BEFORE HE IS DUE TO MAKE A SPEECH AT AN IMPORTANT CONFERENCE WHICH YOU ARE BOTH ATTENDING. WOULD YOU:

A *Leave it to the organisers to deal with the gap in the programme?* ◇

B *Offer to read your boss's speech for him?* ◇

C *Volunteer to address the conference on a different topic?* ◇

Question Seven

THE CHAIRMAN TELLS YOU THAT THE EXPORT SALES DIRECTOR WILL BE RETIRING IN SIX MONTHS' TIME AND THAT YOU ARE A CANDIDATE FOR HIS JOB—PROVIDED THAT YOU CAN LEARN TO SPEAK FRENCH. WOULD YOU:

A *Enrol for an intensive course at a language school, attending in your own time and at your own expense?* ◇

B *Say that you are not interested since you have no gift for languages?* ◇

C *Buy a teach-yourself French book?* ◇

Question Eight

THE PERFORMANCE OF ONE OF YOUR SUBORDINATES BEGINS TO DETERIORATE SHARPLY. WOULD YOU:

A *Do nothing—hoping that he is simply going through a temporary bad patch?* ◇

B *Tell him that you have noticed that he is having difficulties and to let you know if there is anything you can do to help?* ◇

C *Try to find out the reason for his poor performance and jointly agree an improvement plan?* ◇

Question Nine

YOU ARE OFFERED A SUBSTANTIAL PROMOTION, INVOLVING THE ESTABLISHMENT OF A NEW BRANCH OF YOUR FIRM IN A THIRD WORLD COUNTRY WITH A DEMANDING CLIMATE. WOULD YOU:

A *Accept—and begin in-depth research on the economy of the country concerned?* ◇

B *Accept—on condition that you can return to your old job if the new venture doesn't work out?* ◇

C *Decline because you feel that you could not stand the climate?* ◇

Question Ten

YOU RECEIVE AN INVITATION TO ATTEND A COCKTAIL PARTY AT WHICH A NUMBER OF FAMOUS BUSINESSMEN WILL BE PRESENT. WOULD YOU ARRIVE FEELING:

A *Full of dread in case you commit some kind of gaffe?* ◇

B *A little nervous—but excited at the prospect of meeting some interesting people?* ◇

C *Full of confidence that you will be able to hold your own with whoever you may meet?* ◇

CAN YOU PICK TALENTED PEOPLE?

test

FORTY

Spotting potential top managers is a key concern of every progressive company since without such high flyers the future would be bleak. While some experienced executives have an almost uncanny knack of recognising top talent, others are confused and uncertain about what to look for.

Think of an individual in your department whose future you believe to be bright with promise. How would he rate against the following questions—answer Yes or No (*tick for yes, cross for no*)? Does he:

1. *Show enthusiasm for and commitment to the job?* ◇

2. *Inspire, enthuse and motivate his staff?* ◇

3. *Obtain the co-operation of other departments?* ◇

4. *Convert good ideas into outstanding results?* ◇

5. *Set demanding standards for himself and his staff?* ◇

6. *Analyse problems effectively and develop creative solutions?* ◇

101

7. *Make decisions without undue delay?* ◇

8. *Act decisively in complex situations?* ◇

9. *Anticipate the consequences of his decisions?* ◇

10. *Win over others to his point of view?* ◇

11. *See a problem in its broader context?* ◇

12. *Show respect for opposing viewpoints?* ◇

13. *Encourage his staff to contribute ideas and suggestions?* ◇

14. *Develop the work of his group, without being too hidebound by traditional practices?* ◇

15. *Delegate effectively?* ◇

16. *Coach and develop his staff?* ◇

17. *Identify their training needs?* ◇

18. *Keep confidential information to himself?* ◇

19. *Have the stamina for continuous hard work?* ◇

20. *Cope with prolonged periods of stress?* ◇

Is he:

21. *A good listener?* ◇

22. *A good communicator, both orally and in writing?* ◇

23. *Constantly updating his knowledge and skills?* ◇

24. *Sensitive to the role of related departments and willing to help them to overcome their problems?* ◇

25. *Willing to take on additional responsibility when necessary?* ◇

26. *Able to deal effectively with crisis situations?* ◇

27. *Willing to seek help with complex problems?* ◇

28. *Able to recognise where he needs to improve?* ◇

29. *Resilient enough to overcome setbacks?* ◇

30. *Liked and respected by his peers and subordinates?* ◇

31. *Loyal to his boss and colleagues, without being blind to their imperfections?* ◇

32. A member of any professional or management association? ◇

33. Involved in any company sporting or social activities? ◇

34. Prominent in any local community activities? ◇

35. Realistically ambitious, recognising the possible effects upon his personal life? ◇

DO YOU SET GOOD OBJECTIVES?

test

————————FORTY-ONE————————

Hard work and effort are important in management but need to be focused on key objectives instead of being wasted on secondary issues. The ability to set challenging objectives is a primary executive skill—one which determines both the allocation of resources and the direction of effort.

But good objectives do not simply represent vague hopes for the future: they are clear-cut, specific and, wherever possible, measurable. *And they are always written.*

Have you set good objectives for *your* subordinates?— answer Yes or No (*tick for yes, cross for no*).

1. Does each objective start with the word 'to', followed by an action verb? ◇

2. Does it produce a single key result when accomplished? ◇

3. Does it specify a target date for its accomplishment? ◇

4. Is it as specific and measurable as possible? ◇

5. Does it specify only the 'what' and the 'when', not the 'why' and the 'how'? ◇

6. Is it directly related to the subordinate's key responsibilities as set out in his job description? ◇

7. Is it tough and demanding but nevertheless realistic and attainable? ◇

103

8. *Is it consistent with the resources available or anticipated?* ◇

9. *Is it consistent with basic company and organisational policies and practices?* ◇

10. *Will the result, when achieved, justify the expenditure of time and resource required to achieve it?* ◇

11. *Where co-operation with others is required to achieve the objective, does it specify who is accountable for the final result?* ◇

12. *Are you satisfied that your subordinate clearly understands each of his objectives?* ◇

13. *Were the objectives jointly agreed in discussions between yourself and your subordinate, without undue pressure on your part?* ◇

14. *Have you given your subordinate a copy of his objectives?* ◇

15. *Have you agreed with him the frequency of future meetings to review progress?* ◇

ARE YOU A GOOD LISTENER?

test

---FORTY-TWO---

Research has shown that many executives spend up to 50% of their time listening to other people. An executive who doesn't listen properly makes mistakes and gets out of touch.

The keys to effective listening are concentration and self-discipline. Instead of sitting back and letting the speaker do all the work, become an *active* listener—you'll find it much more rewarding.

Let's assume that you have been invited to attend a talk. This test may show you where you need to improve.

———————————Do you:———————————

1. *Sit where you can see the speaker and hear him comfortably?*

    A Yes ◇   B No ◇

2. *Allow yourself to be distracted by his personality or appearance?*

    A Yes ◇   B No ◇

3. *Decide early on that the subject is too difficult and that you'll never understand it?*

    A Yes ◇   B No ◇

4. *Stop listening because you disagree with the speaker?*

    A Yes ◇   B No ◇

5. *Hear only what you want or expect to hear?*

    A Yes ◇   B No ◇

6. *Constantly daydream—while faking attention?*

    A Yes ◇   B No ◇

7. *'Switch off' from boredom or because you think you know it already?*

    A Yes ◇   B No ◇

8. *Listen only for facts and not ideas?*

    A Yes ◇   B No ◇

9. *Make mental summaries of each main stage of the talk?*

    A Yes ◇   B No ◇

10. *Mentally list the points for and against the speaker's arguments?*

    A Yes ◇   B No ◇

11. *Listen for what the speaker doesn't say—'read between the lines'?*

    A Yes ◇   B No ◇

12. *Take notes of any points which it is important that you remember?*

    A Yes ◇   B No ◇

13. *Note down any questions which you intend to ask during the question period?*

    A *Yes* ◇ **B** *No* ◇

14. *Give the speaker some visual feedback (smile at his humour, nod in agreement, frown if confused, etc.)?*

    A *Yes* ◇ **B** *No* ◇

15. *Recognise that even a poor speaker may have an important message?*

    A *Yes* ◇ **B** *No* ◇

WHAT MATTERS TO YOU MOST IN YOUR WORK?

test

—————— FORTY-THREE ——————

Different jobs provide different satisfactions for different individuals. If what the job offers matches what the individual needs the stage is set for good performance; if not, the most likely outcome is apathy and frustration.

The question is: how well do you know yourself? Which needs and values are most important to you in your work? Below is a list of factors that can provide job satisfaction. Rate yourself and discover what makes you tick.

1. A good and stable level of pay.

    Important ◇ *Fairly important* ◇ *Not important* ◇

2. Guaranteed increments within a pay scale.

    Important ◇ *Fairly important* ◇ *Not important* ◇

3. Pleasant working conditions.

    Important ◇ *Fairly important* ◇ *Not important* ◇

4. Good fringe benefits.

    Important ◇ *Fairly important* ◇ *Not important* ◇

5. Good job security.

    Important ◇   *Fairly important* ◇   *Not important* ◇

6. Congenial colleagues.

    Important ◇   *Fairly important* ◇   *Not important* ◇

7. A considerate boss.

    Important ◇   *Fairly important* ◇   *Not important* ◇

8. A clear job description.

    Important ◇   *Fairly important* ◇   *Not important* ◇

9. Clear policies and procedures.

    Important ◇   *Fairly important* ◇   *Not important* ◇

10. A steady pace of work.

    Important ◇   *Fairly important* ◇   *Not important* ◇

11. Moderate technological change.

    Important ◇   *Fairly important* ◇   *Not important* ◇

12. Little prolonged stress.

    Important ◇   *Fairly important* ◇   *Not important* ◇

13. Good employee communications.

    Important ◇   *Fairly important* ◇   *Not important* ◇

14. Good social/sporting facilities.

    Important ◇   *Fairly important* ◇   *Not important* ◇

15. Promotion by seniority.

    Important ◇   *Fairly important* ◇   *Not important* ◇

16. A high level of pay, with profit sharing, bonuses, etc.

    Important ◇   *Fairly important* ◇   *Not important* ◇

17. A challenging job in a competitive environment.

    Important ◇   *Fairly important* ◇   *Not important* ◇

18. Plenty of variety, with a high level of technological change.

    Important ◇   *Fairly important* ◇   *Not important* ◇   **107**

19. A demanding boss.

     Important ◇   *Fairly important* ◇   *Not important* ◇

20. Freedom to use initiative.

     Important ◇   *Fairly important* ◇   *Not important* ◇

21. Minimum bureaucracy.

     Important ◇   *Fairly important* ◇   *Not important* ◇

22. Recognition for good work.

     Important ◇   *Fairly important* ◇   *Not important* ◇

23. Excellent promotion opportunities.

     Important ◇   *Fairly important* ◇   *Not important* ◇

24. An expanding organisation.

     Important ◇   *Fairly important* ◇   *Not important* ◇

25. An impressive office.

     Important ◇   *Fairly important* ◇   *Not important* ◇

26. A prestige car.

     Important ◇   *Fairly important* ◇   *Not.important* ◇

27. Participation in decision-making.

     Important ◇   *Fairly important* ◇   *Not important* ◇

28. Promotion on merit.

     Important ◇   *Fairly important* ◇   *Not important* ◇

29. Minimum supervision.

     Important ◇   *Fairly important* ◇   *Not important* ◇

30. Wide range of contacts.

     Important ◇   *Fairly important* ◇   *Not important* ◇

CAN YOU MOTIVATE PEOPLE?

test

FORTY-FOUR

Motivating subordinates to achieve high standards of performance is one of the most exacting requirements of the executive's job. Success depends largely upon whether he can adapt his own natural style of managing to different individuals and different situations. An inflexible approach is a recipe for disaster.

This test poses a number of real-life problems which are capable of being dealt with in several different ways—none of which is intrinsically superior to the others. It will show you your own preferred management style and indicate what other options might be considered.

Question One

YOU ARE PLANNING A RADICAL RE-ORGANISATION OF YOUR DEPARTMENT AS PART OF A NEW OPERATIONAL STRATEGY. WOULD YOU:

A *Give priority to the needs of the organisation?*

B *Give priority to the needs of your staff?*

C *Try to achieve a balance between both?*

Question Two

TO WHAT EXTENT WOULD YOU INVOLVE YOUR SUBORDINATES IN DETERMINING THE NEW STRATEGY? WOULD YOU:

A *Keep their involvement to the minimum—seeing the decision as your personal responsibility?*

B *Involve them completely and arrive at decisions by consensus?*

C *Consult them individually and then make your decision?*

Question Three

ASSUME THAT THE STRATEGY HAS BEEN AGREED AND IS NOW BEING IMPLEMENTED. WOULD YOU:

A *Involve yourself continuously—issuing instructions, checking on progress and taking any necessary corrective actions?*

B *Give most of your attention to maintaining staff morale and deal with any problems which are causing them concern?*

C *Leave them to get on with the strategy, having made* ◇
sure that everyone understands what he has to do?

---Question Four---

YOUR DEPARTMENT IS ASSIGNED A MAJOR
PROJECT WHICH INVOLVES LIAISING WITH MANY
DIFFERENT GROUPS AND LEVELS OF
MANAGEMENT. IN CONSIDERING WHICH OF YOUR
SUBORDINATES SHOULD UNDERTAKE SPECIFIC
TASKS, WOULD YOU:

A *Be guided entirely by your assessment of each* ◇
individual's skills and abilities?

B *Discuss the problem with your subordinates and arrive* ◇
at a mutually-agreed allocation of tasks?

C *Weigh the needs of the project against the* ◇
opportunities it offers for personal development and,
wherever possible, assign individuals to tasks which
will broaden their experience?

---Question Five---

WHEN SELECTING A CANDIDATE FOR A JUNIOR
MANAGEMENT VACANCY IN YOUR GROUP,
WOULD YOU GIVE MOST EMPHASIS TO:

A *Whether he had the knowledge and skills to do the* ◇
immediate job?

B *Whether he would be likely to find the job personally* ◇
satisfying?

C *His potential for further advancement?* ◇

---Question Six---

WHEN APPRAISING THE PERFORMANCE OF YOUR
STAFF, WHICH OF THE FOLLOWING FACTORS DO
YOU FEEL ARE MOST IMPORTANT:

A *The results achieved?* ◇

B *The ability to get along with all types of people?* ◇

C *The ability to get results with the willing co-operation* ◇
of others who are involved?

---Question Seven---

SUPPOSE THAT ONE OF YOUR SUBORDINATES
MADE A SERIOUS MISTAKE WHICH CAUSED YOU

CONSIDERABLE EMBARRASSMENT. WOULD YOU:

A *Reprimand the individual concerned and spell out the consequences should it happen again?* ◇

B *Discuss the matter with him as gently as possible so as not to undermine his self-confidence and morale?* ◇

C *Analyse constructively what went wrong and develop a plan to prevent similar mistakes in the future?* ◇

----------------------Question Eight----------------------
YOU DEVELOP A STRONG DISLIKE FOR A NEW COLLEAGUE WITH WHOM YOU HAVE TO WORK CLOSELY. WOULD YOU:

A *Make your feelings very clear to him, either directly or indirectly?* ◇

B *See it as a challenge and try to make friends with him?* ◇

C *Keep your relationship on a strictly impersonal 'business' basis?* ◇

----------------------Question Nine----------------------
ONE OF THE BRIGHTEST PEOPLE IN YOUR DEPARTMENT—SOMEONE YOU REGARD AS A PROTÉGÉ—RESIGNS TO JOIN A COMPETITOR. WOULD YOU:

A *Express your disappointment at what you regard as an act of disloyalty—to you and to the company?* ◇

B *Wish him every success in his new job and assure him that he can rely upon you to give him a good reference?* ◇

C *Accept his decision, find out what assignments are outstanding and ensure that he briefs his successor before leaving?* ◇

----------------------Question Ten----------------------
WHAT IS YOUR PREFERRED METHOD OF COMMUNICATING WITH YOUR SUBORDINATES? DO YOU PREFER TO:

A *Communicate with them individually, keeping group meetings to the minimum?* ◇

B *Hold frequent group meetings?* ◇

C *Communicate both individually and at meetings, depending upon the issue involved?* ◇

HOW DETERMINED ARE YOU?

FORTY-FIVE

There are times when every executive must be prepared to fight for what he believes in—to stick to his guns in the teeth of opposition. Without such determination good ideas would be lost and organisations would cease to grow.

How do *you* react when you are challenged or opposed? Here are some situations to test your mettle.

Question One

YOU ARE MAKING A MAJOR PRESENTATION AT A MANAGEMENT MEETING. ONE OF YOUR COLLEAGUES LAUNCHES A FIERCE ATTACK UPON YOUR PROPOSAL. WOULD YOU:

A *Try to pacify him by conceding that some of his comments may be justified?* ◇

B *Look upset and protest that he has misunderstood you?* ◇

C *Hit back forcefully and try to rebut his criticisms?* ◇

Question Two

DURING AN APPRAISAL INTERVIEW YOUR BOSS MAKES WHAT YOU FEEL IS AN UNJUSTIFIED CRITICISM. WOULD YOU:

A *Say nothing but grin and bear it?* ◇

B *Challenge him immediately and try to persuade him that he is mistaken?* ◇

C *Disagree but promise to consider what he has said?* ◇

Question Three

AN INDIVIDUAL WITH A REPUTATION FOR BEING EXTREMELY DIFFICULT TO MANAGE IS ASSIGNED TO YOUR DEPARTMENT. WOULD YOU:

A *Avoid him as much as possible and turn a blind eye to his indiscretions?* ◇

B *Tell him that you expect his full co-operation or you will take steps to remove him?* ◇

C *Welcome him to your group but tell him that you'll be keeping an eye on him?* ◇

—————————————Question Four—————————————

AFTER MONTHS OF PREPARATION YOU ARE ABOUT TO EMBARK ON A MAJOR PROJECT. AT THE LAST MOMENT YOU ARE TOLD THAT YOUR BUDGET IS TO BE CUT. WOULD YOU:

A *Demand an explanation and argue as hard as possible for the cuts to be withdrawn?* ◇

B *Protest but agree to operate on the reduced budget?* ◇

C *Accept the cuts but point out that success is now highly unlikely?* ◇

—————————————Question Five—————————————

YOU FIND THAT SOMEONE ELSE HAS PARKED IN YOUR RESERVED SPACE AT THE OFFICE CAR PARK. WOULD YOU:

A *Confront the owner of the car and ask him to remove it?* ◇

B *Report the incident to the security staff and ask them to take action?* ◇

C *Look for another space?* ◇

—————————————Question Six—————————————

YOU FEEL THAT YOUR SALARY IS TOO LOW AND THAT YOU DESERVE A SPECIAL INCREASE. WOULD YOU:

A *Mention it to your boss and ask him to consider it?* ◇

B *Do nothing—but tell all your friends how unhappy you are?* ◇

C *Argue your case forcefully with your boss, threatening to leave unless he agrees?* ◇

—————————————Question Seven—————————————

A SUPPLIER DELIVERS A BATCH OF FAULTY COMPONENTS WHICH HOLDS UP WORK IN YOUR DEPARTMENT. THE M.D. OF THE SUPPLYING FIRM IS A FRIEND OF YOUR OWN M.D. WOULD YOU:

A Return the components to the supplier and request replacements? ◇

B Demand immediate replacements plus compensation for loss of production? ◇

C Inform your boss and ask him how you should handle it? ◇

Question Eight
YOU DISCOVER THAT A KEY MEMBER OF YOUR GROUP HAS BEEN CHEATING ON HIS EXPENSE ACCOUNT. WOULD YOU:

A Warn him that strong action will be taken if he ever does it again? ◇

B Severely reprimand him and arrange for the money to be repaid from his next salary cheque? ◇

C Inform your boss and leave it to him to decide what to do? ◇

Question Nine
AFTER A TIRING CAR JOURNEY YOU ARRIVE FOR AN APPOINTMENT WITH AN IMPORTANT CUSTOMER ONLY TO FIND THAT HIS SECRETARY HAS FORGOTTEN TO NOTE IT IN HIS DIARY. THE CUSTOMER IS NOW AT ANOTHER MEETING. WOULD YOU:

A Accept the secretary's apologies and make another appointment? ◇

B Ask her to explain to her boss what has happened and to find out whether he can see you? ◇

C Phone him the next day to complain? ◇

Question Ten
YOUR BOSS TURNS DOWN A PROPOSAL WHICH YOU ARE CONVINCED WOULD ENABLE YOUR PRODUCT TO PENETRATE NEW MARKETS AND EARN GOOD PROFITS. WOULD YOU:

A Go over his head and seek an interview with his boss? ◇

B Forget the whole thing? ◇

C Accept the decision temporarily—but start working on other ways to convince him? ◇

CAN YOU HANDLE SOCIAL EVENTS?

FORTY-SIX

From time to time every executive finds himself attending social functions: formal dinners, cocktail parties, company outings and dances, awards for long service or outstanding performance. Each of these situations gives him an opportunity to project his personality and to practise various social skills. But despite the relaxed atmosphere he is still very much on duty and it is important that he makes a good impression.

How comfortable are you on such occasions? Do you make your presence felt or simply melt into the background? Answer Yes or No (*tick for yes, cross for no*).

1. *Do you welcome invitations to social functions?* ◇

2. *Do you like meeting new people from different backgrounds?* ◇

3. *Do you take the initiative in introducing yourself to strangers?* ◇

4. *Do you enjoy finding out about their interests?* ◇

5. *Are you embarrassed by questions about your own background and interests?* ◇

6. *Are you comfortable exchanging small talk with people you don't know?* ◇

7. *Do you enjoy 'dressing up' on formal occasions?* ◇

8. *Would you accept an invitation to make an after-dinner speech?* ◇

9. *Would you welcome an opportunity to organise a major company social function?* ◇

10. *Would you welcome an opportunity to act as M.C.?* ◇

11. *Are you put off by people with accents very different from your own?* ◇

115

12. *Do you feel that your own speech sometimes lets you down?* ◇

13. *Do you become bored with foreigners who speak little English?* ◇

14. *Do you like to take the lead in initiating topics of conversation?* ◇

15. *Do you like to be the centre of attention at office parties?* ◇

16. *Do you associate easily with people junior to yourself?* ◇

17. *Do you expect them to show respect for your higher status?* ◇

18. *Do you tend to drink heavily at functions where alcohol is plentiful?* ◇

19. *Have you ever been guilty of a lapse of good taste while under the influence of alcohol?* ◇

20. *Do you enjoy proposing a toast or a vote of thanks?* ◇

21. *At a company outing or sports day, would you mind looking silly in the cause of good fun?* ◇

22. *Would you be prepared to play Santa Claus at a children's party?* ◇

ARE YOU EFFICIENT?

FORTY-SEVEN

To be recognised as efficient is one of the highest accolades that any executive can have. Essentially, it means that he runs a well-organised, cost-effective operation which maximises resources and gets results. To do this he needs to be both a leader and an organiser and to demonstrate a talent for thinking ahead.

Does *your* efficiency make you stand out from the crowd? See how you fare with the following questions (*tick for yes, cross for no*):

THE JOB

1. *Do you have a clear, up to date job description?* ◇

2. *Have you devised your short and long-term work objectives?* ◇

3. *Have you discussed and agreed them with your boss?* ◇

4. *Do your objectives have agreed target dates and criteria by which success and progress can be measured?* ◇

5. *Have you translated your objectives into specific work programmes?* ◇

6. *Do you have a clear understanding of your priority tasks?* ◇

7. *Have you briefed your subordinates on these objectives and plans and gained their commitment?* ◇

8. *Do they have clear job descriptions and work objectives?* ◇

9. *Is your work team organised in the best possible way, building on the strengths of its individual members?* ◇

10. *Do you carry out regular progress reviews with your staff and adjust their objectives and targets where necessary?* ◇

11. *Do you check quality standards regularly and constantly strive to improve them?* ◇

12. *Do you think and plan well ahead, especially for contingencies?* ◇

13. *Do you review and revise your plans as needs arise and inform your staff accordingly?* ◇

14. *Do you constantly update your knowledge and skills?* ◇

15. *Could you stand in for your boss and deputise effectively during his absence?* ◇

THE WORK TEAM

16. *Do you set high standards of performance and ensure that they are achieved?* ◇

17. *Do you hold regular group meetings to review*

progress, seek ideas and opinions, make plans and obtain feedback? ◇

18. Do you actively encourage group spirit and teamwork? ◇

19. Do you delegate effectively? ◇

20. Have you built a good sense of group self-discipline? ◇

21. Do you keep your people well informed of changes in company policies and procedures and explain the reasons for such changes? ◇

22. Do you use each individual's abilities to the full? ◇

————DEVELOPING INDIVIDUALS————

23. Do you make positive efforts to get to know each member of your staff? ◇

24. Are you approachable to everyone? ◇

25. Have you assessed each individual's training needs and developed realistic training? ◇

26. Do you appraise your staff regularly? ◇

27. Do you deal quickly and effectively with human relations problems? ◇

28. Have you identified a potential successor for each key job in your group? ◇

29. Do you promote individuals strictly on merit? ◇

30. Do you make a point of praising subordinates for a job well done? ◇

ARE YOU DOMINANT?

————FORTY-EIGHT————

Every successful executive must know how to command attention and respect, otherwise he would make no impact upon the organisation. Yet too much aggression can be counter-productive, giving the over-dominant individual the wrong kind of image and causing others to be reluctant to communicate with him.

Are you dominant—or domineering? Do you roar like a lion, squeak like a mouse or make whatever noises seem appropriate at the time?

1. *Do you speak in a loud voice?*

    Frequently ◇   Sometimes ◇   Never ◇

2. *When the chairman of a meeting calls for questions or comments, are you among the first to contribute?*

    Always ◇   Occasionally ◇   Never ◇

3. *Do you 'blow your top' when you discover silly mistakes?*

    Frequently ◇   Sometimes ◇   Never ◇

4. *Do you express strong opinions about the competence of your colleagues and subordinates?*

    Frequently ◇   Occasionally ◇   Never ◇

5. *Do you ever use sarcasm when criticising others?*

    Frequently ◇   Occasionally ◇   Never ◇

6. *Do you use swear words in your ordinary conversation?*

    Frequently ◇   Occasionally ◇   Never ◇

7. *Do you interrupt your subordinates when they are trying to explain something to you?*

    Frequently ◇   Sometimes ◇   Rarely ◇

8. *Do you ever use your senior status to intimidate more junior people?*

    Frequently ◇   Occasionally ◇   Never ◇

9. *When a colleague has done something which has annoyed you, have you ever stormed into his office to 'give him a piece of your mind'?*

    Often ◇   Occasionally ◇   Never ◇

10. *How important are status symbols to you (large office, prestige car, etc.)?*

    Very important ◇   Important ◇   Not very important ◇

11. Do you believe that 'attack is the best form of defence'—and act accordingly when you are criticised?

Yes ◇

Occasionally—but I believe it's better to listen and remain calm. ◇

Never—it's not my style. ◇

12. Do you enjoy exercising your authority over your subordinates—issuing instructions, giving reprimands, appraising their performance, deciding upon their salary increases?

Yes—it is a major source of job satisfaction. ◇

Not particularly—I get more satisfaction from building a good team. ◇

No—I find such things very worrying. ◇

13. When you have a tough problem to resolve, do you ever seek the advice of experienced colleagues or subordinates?

Very rarely—I consider it a sign of weakness. ◇

Frequently—they often come up with some excellent ideas. ◇

Always—their ideas are usually so much better than mine. ◇

14. When you become bored at a meeting or with a speaker, do you show it openly, e.g. by frequent yawning, doodling or drumming your fingers on the table?

Frequently—I resent my time being wasted. ◇

Only very rarely. ◇

Never—I daydream instead. ◇

15. Do you become impatient with people who seem to have difficulty in understanding your instructions or ideas?

Frequently ◇   Occasionally ◇   Never—I am used to it. ◇

16. Have you ever slammed the door as you walked out of a room after an argument with a colleague?

Often ◇   Only very rarely ◇   Never ◇

17. Have you ever terminated an argument on the telephone by slamming down the receiver?

Often ◇   Only very rarely ◇   Never ◇

18. *Do you believe that a speaker who makes a poor presentation deserves to be publicly humiliated?*

Yes—he will take more care next time. ◇

Only if he was deliberately trying to mislead the audience. ◇

No ◇

19. *Have you ever reprimanded a subordinate for wearing what you considered to be unsuitable clothing or an unacceptable hair style?*

Often ◇   Only very rarely ◇   Never ◇

20. *Have you ever threatened to fire someone?*

Often ◇   Only very rarely ◇   Never ◇

DO YOU HAVE A GOOD MEMORY?

test

FORTY-NINE

A good memory is essential for any successful executive. Despite the continuing advances in information technology, most data is stored in the human memory, available for recall when the occasion demands. To be able to 'tap into' his memory, quickly and easily, is a most impressive executive talent. By contrast a memory which functions badly can project an image of personal inefficiency.

Is your memory as good as you think it is?

1. *Do you forget to note appointments in your diary?*

Frequently ◇   Sometimes ◇   Never ◇

2. *Are you surprised by the arrival of visitors whose appointments you have forgotten?*

Frequently ◇   Sometimes ◇   Never ◇

3. *Do you receive reminders from your secretary that you are late for meetings which you have forgotten?*

    Frequently ◇   Sometimes ◇   Never ◇

4. *Do you go into meetings and discover that you have left important papers behind in your office?*

    Frequently ◇   Sometimes ◇   Never ◇

5. *When you are contributing to discussions at meetings, do you ever start a sentence and then forget your point?*

    Frequently ◇   Sometimes ◇   Never ◇

6. *When people from other departments greet you in the office, do you have difficulty in putting names to faces?*

    Frequently ◇   Sometimes ◇   Never ◇

7. *When you are introduced to someone at a business function, do you forget his name within a few minutes?*

    Frequently ◇   Sometimes ◇   Never ◇

8. *Have you ever forgotten to meet a customer or colleague at an airport or railway station?*

    Frequently ◇   Sometimes ◇   Never ◇

9. *Have you ever run out of petrol when driving to work?*

    Frequently ◇   Sometimes ◇   Never ◇

10. *Do you forget to ring your wife when you have to work late at the office?*

    Frequently ◇   Sometimes ◇   Never ◇

11. *Do you ever forget where you parked your car in the office car park?*

    Frequently ◇   Sometimes ◇   Never ◇

12. *Have you ever discovered that you have forgotten to bring your notes and/or visual aids just before you are due to give an important presentation?*

    Frequently ◇   Sometimes ◇   Never ◇

13. *Have you ever 'dried up' in the middle of a presentation because you couldn't remember what your next point was?*

Frequently ◇   Sometimes ◇   Never ◇

14. *Do you forget to send Christmas cards to important business contacts?*

      Frequently ◇   Sometimes ◇   Never ◇

15. *Do you forget to send a card on your secretary's birthday?*

      Frequently ◇   Sometimes ◇   Never ◇

16. *Do you forget the office telephone numbers of your immediate subordinates?*

      Frequently ◇   Sometimes ◇   Never ◇

17. *Do you forget the first names of the wives, husbands or partners of your immediate subordinates?*

      Frequently ◇   Sometimes ◇   Never ◇

18. *Do your subordinates have to remind you that you have forgotten to review their salaries?*

      Frequently ◇   Sometimes ◇   Never ◇

19. *Do you forget to appraise your subordinates?*

      Frequently ◇   Sometimes ◇   Never ◇

20. *Have you ever forgotten to congratulate a colleague or subordinate on being promoted?*

      Frequently ◇   Sometimes ◇   Never ◇

ARE YOU IN THE RIGHT JOB?

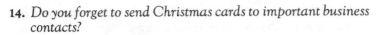

test FIFTY

The fact that a person is an executive does not necessarily mean that he is finding satisfaction in his work—or even that he has chosen the right career. Each year hundreds of bored or frustrated executives drop out of their jobs and take up a completely different type of work—perhaps one which is connected with an absorbing hobby. Thousands more like their jobs well enough but change their employers, seeking more money, more status or greater opportunities for advancement.

Have *you* found the right niche—or is your job a bed of nails? Answer Yes or No (*tick for yes, cross for no*).

1. *Did you always plan to do the kind of work you are now doing?* ◇

2. *Has your career proved as satisfying as you hoped it would be?* ◇

3. *If you could put the clock back, would you still choose the same career?* ◇

4. *Would you encourage your children to take up your kind of work?* ◇

5. *Do you feel that your job makes good use of your natural abilities?* ◇

6. *Are your educational qualifications and/or professional training relevant to your present job?* ◇

7. *Does your job give you the opportunity to increase your knowledge and skills?* ◇

8. *Is there plenty of variety in your work?* ◇

9. *Do you look forward to going to work in the morning?* ◇

10. *Are you generally one of the first people to arrive at the office?* ◇

11. *Are you usually one of the last to leave in the evening?* ◇

12. *Do you generally arrive home feeling that you have done a good job?* ◇

13. *Do you bring work home in the evenings or at weekends?* ◇

14. *Do you enjoy talking about your job outside working hours?* ◇

15. *Are you glad to get back to your job after having taken a holiday?* ◇

16. *If you were to leave your present job, would you look for the same kind of work in another organisation?* ◇

17. *Do you get along with your boss?*

18. *Do you find the majority of your colleagues congenial?*

19. *Do you socialise with them outside the office?*

20. *Are you clear about the objectives of your job?*

21. *Do you feel that you have sufficient authority to do your job?*

22. *Are you generally satisfied with your income?*

23. *Does your job have good promotion prospects?*

24. *Are the fringe benefits satisfactory?*

25. *Do you feel reasonably secure in your job?*

26. *Do you feel that your abilities are appreciated?*

27. *Is there a friendly atmosphere in your company?*

28. *Do you take part in company social functions or sporting activities?*

29. *Do you consider your company to be a good employer?*

30. *Would you recommend the company to job-seeking friends or acquaintances?*

31. *Do you feel worn out at the end of the day?*

32. *Do you lie awake at night worrying about your job?*

33. *Are you frequently late for work?*

34. *Do you often find yourself taking extended lunch breaks?*

35. *Are you always looking for opportunities to spend time away from the office?*

36. *Do you regard casual visitors who drop in for a chat as providing a welcome break from your work?*

37. *Do you ever feign illness to avoid going to work?*

38. *Do you find that alcohol helps you to cope with the stresses of your job?*

39. *Are you taking tranquillisers to calm your nerves?*

40. *Are you actively looking for another job?*

ANSWERS

TEST 1

Question:

	1.	2.	3.	4.
	A 0	A 10	A 10	A 0
	B 10	B 5	B 5	B 5
	C 5	C 0	C 0	C 10
	5.	6.	7.	8.	9.
	A 0	A 10	A 5	A 0	A 10
	B 10	B 0	B 0	B 10	B 5
	C 5	C 5	C 10	C 5	C 0
	10.		
	A 5	B 10	C 0

SCORE 80–100

You are an excellent leader who knows how to motivate people to give of their best. Any group led by you will exhibit high levels of trust and commitment.

SCORE 55–75

You have a positive attitude to managing people and major errors of judgment are rare. Occasionally you could be more adventurous.

SCORE 25–50

You are much too cautious and are tending to stifle your subordinates' development. Try to have more confidence in yourself—and in other people.

SCORE 0–20

You shouldn't be in charge of people at all.

TEST 2

Give yourself 5 points for every YES answer.

SCORE 60–80

You are a highly professional executive who actively manages his own development. For you change is welcome and exciting.

SCORE 40–55

You have a positive attitude to change but could push yourself a little harder to keep up with new developments.

SCORE 20–35

You are in danger of becoming out of date. Act quickly and set yourself some really challenging goals.

SCORE 0–15

You have a great deal of catching-up to do.

TEST 3

Question:

	1.	2.	3.	4.
	A 10	A 5	A 0	A 0
	B 0	B 10	B 10	B 10
	C 5	C 0	C 5	C 5
	5.	6.	7.	8.	9.
	A 5	A 10	A 5	A 10	A 0
	B 10	B 0	B 10	B 5	B 10
	C 0	C 5	C 0	C 0	C 5
	10.		
	A 10	B 0	C 5

SCORE 80–100

You are an extremely confident executive who believes in seizing the initiative. Be careful, though, that you are not seen as *too* domineering. A little tact will go a long, long way.

SCORE 55–75

You have plenty of self-confidence and can cope with most situations. Occasionally, you find discretion the better part of valour.

SCORE 25–50

You are too concerned with what might go wrong and are probably seen as excessively cautious. Try to be more assertive—life without risk would be dull indeed!

SCORE 0–20

You are giving an excellent impression of the Invisible Man! It's hard to see how you would survive if ever the company decided it needed fewer executives.

TEST 4

Score 1 point for every YES.

SCORE 13–15

You are an outstanding team leader

who works hard to keep everyone moving in the right direction. No doubt you are rewarded by some superb results.

SCORE 8–12

You have a firm grasp of the essentials of team leadership but could be more systematic in a few areas.

SCORE 4–7

You are unlikely to get the best out of your group until you put yourself in their place and start asking yourself how *you* would expect to be treated by an effective team leader.

SCORE 0–3

Whatever your other talents, generating team spirit is certainly not one of them. You are better at working with things than with people.

————————TEST 5————————

Give yourself 5 points for every YES.

SCORE 60–75

You are a thoroughly systematic delegator who uses delegation as a powerful motivational tool.

SCORE 40–55

Generally you do a good job, though your tendency towards perfectionism sometimes prevents you from being more adventurous.

SCORE 15–35

You are overlooking several important points. Use this test as a checklist and start working on your weaknesses. Try to show more trust and confidence in your people.

SCORE 0–10

You hardly ever delegate and when you do, you do it badly. To go on as you are is a certain recipe for chronic fatigue—and for a breakdown in your health.

————————TEST 6————————

Give yourself 5 points for every YES answer.

SCORE 60–75

You are an excellent developer of people—a virtual one-man business school! People fortunate enough to work for you have every opportunity to develop their talents.

SCORE 40–55

You are a sound enough developer but need to be a shade more imaginative in your choice of methods. Look upon every discussion with your subordinates as a potential coaching opportunity.

SCORE 15–35

You are not sufficiently involved in developing your staff and are probably relying too heavily upon formal courses. Unless you make a bigger personal effort your own career ambitions may be jeopardised, as it may be difficult to release you if you have failed to train a successor.

SCORE 0–10

You are risking being relieved of your man-management responsibilities since you are shamefully neglecting your most precious asset. Being assigned to work for you must seem like the kiss of death to any ambitious individual.

————————TEST 7————————

Status-consciousness is measured by the number of (**A**) answers.

If you answered (**A**) to 13 or more questions, then you are extremely status-conscious—the sort of man who looks down upon those beneath him and grovels to those in more senior positions.

If you scored 7–12 you are still notably status-conscious and do not find it easy to relax with those below you. Occasionally, however, you unbend a little.

If you scored 3–6 you are only rarely smitten by the status bug and like to think of yourself as 'one of the boys'.

If you scored 2 or less, then what on earth are you doing in business—you are clearly a candidate for sainthood!

————————TEST 8————————

Question:	1. A 5	2. A 0	3. A 10	4. A 0
	B 0	B 5	B 0	B 10
	C 10	C 10	C 5	C 5
	5. A 10	6. A 5	7. A 0	8. A 10	9. A 10
	B 5	B 0	B 10	B 0	B 5
	C 0	C 10	C 5	C 5	C 0
	10. A 5	B 10	C 0		

SCORE 80–100

You are a mature and perceptive appraiser who can be relied upon to assess people fairly and to handle them sensitively.

SCORE 50–75
Competent and sincere, you need only a slightly more relaxed approach to become a top-flight appraiser. Apply for a refresher training course to refine your skills.

SCORE 20–45
You have a number of weaknesses which you should start working on right away. Seek the advice of an experienced colleague or of your personnel and training manager. You need intensive basic training in appraisal skills.

SCORE 0–15
No wonder talented people dislike working for you!

-----------------TEST 9-----------------
5 marks for each correct answer.

1. B	6. C	11. A
2. B	7. B	12. A
3. C	8. A	13. C
4. A	9. B	14. A
5. B	10. B	15. C

SCORE 60–75
You are very much in touch with what's new in management—and are determined to remain ahead of the pack. Your breadth of knowledge is highly commendable.

SCORE 40–55
You recognise the need to keep up-to-date but a more sustained effort could pay even greater dividends. Make sure that you read *at least* one first-class management journal every month.

SCORE 20–35
The management scene is changing but you are not changing with it. Decide where your priority needs lie and pursue them vigorously—there is no time to lose.

SCORE 0–15
R.I.P.

-----------------TEST 10-----------------
For each FREQUENTLY give yourself 4 points;
For each SOMETIMES give yourself 3 points;
For each RARELY give yourself 2 points;
For each NEVER give yourself 1 point.

SCORE 50 +
You are an out-and-out ditherer who must be the despair of everyone who works with you or for you. You really cannot expect to go on like this—right now you must be one of the most dispensable people on your company's payroll.

SCORE 40–49
You are scarcely a Herculean figure either but at least you do occasionally display some moral courage. Take heart from your successes and remember that being decisive is a lot more satisfying than always seeking to put off the evil day.

SCORE 30–39
You deal confidently with most situations, with only occasional moments of indecisiveness.

SCORE 15–29
You enjoy taking decisions and do not allow yourself to be sidetracked by either complexity or politics. You set an excellent example to your subordinates.

-----------------TEST 11-----------------
Count 1 point for every answer which agrees with this table:

1. A	2. B	3. B	4. A	5. B
6. A	7. A	8. A	9. A	10. B
11. A	12. A	13. B	14. A	15. B

SCORE 13–15
It takes an excellent manager to produce people who are as good or even better than himself. You are such a manager.

SCORE 8–12
Most high-flyers will enjoy working for you, though some may find you a shade too conservative.

SCORE 3–7
You are tending to regard the high-flyer as a nuisance rather than a challenge. Give him more of your time and recognise that his successes will be seen partly as a tribute to the way you are managing him.

SCORE 0–2
You are a menace to the future prosperity of your company. No high-flyer worth his salt will long endure being managed by someone from whom he has so little to learn.

-----------------TEST 12-----------------
Give yourself 5 points for every YES answer:

SCORE 60–75
You are an extremely well organised executive who knows that good working habits save time and reduce stress.

SCORE 35–55
Your carelessness sometimes creates problems for yourself and others, though these are more irritating than catastrophic. Greater self-discipline would do your image a power of good.

SCORE 30 or less
You are wasting an awful lot of time by failing to organise yourself and your work. People will undoubtedly be losing their respect for you. You really are asking for trouble if you go on like this.

------------TEST 13------------
Each correct answer wins FIVE POINTS.

1. **C** The beginning is a vital stage. Members need to know why the meeting has been called, what is expected of them and what constraints may apply to their discussions (e.g. whether they can authorise expenditure and, if so, how much).

2. **A** If you have an expert, use him early on so that the group gets the benefit of his knowledge and experience. Having done so, give the other members an opportunity to air their views and don't let the expert continue to dominate.

3. **C** You must recognise the point when a hitherto healthy debate is about to turn into a brawl and move quickly to assert your authority. The longer you delay, the more your credibility will suffer.

4. **B** There's an easy way and a hard way of dealing with such people. Take the easy way first—if it doesn't work (and it usually does) then any firmer action will have the support of the whole group.

5. **C** Sometimes you come across bright people who are very shy in meetings and are perfectly happy to remain silent. Getting them to contribute is like trying to coax a pet bird to return to its cage: you must be gentle or your quarry will panic!

6. **A** As the senior person present, you are already in a dominant position. If you appear to exploit it by monopolising the discussion too, then people will simply 'turn off' and wonder why you bothered to call the meeting.

7. **B** You must maintain law and order at all times. Recognise that you can only handle one issue at a time and insist upon a disciplined approach, without losing your temper. Such firmness wins respect whereas being too soft simply encourages anarchy.

8. **C** Always ensure everyone knows what has been decided at each stage of the meeting before going on to the next. To leave all the decisions and action points to the end, when everyone is likely to be tired, is to risk confusion and misunderstanding.

9. **B** It's always tempting to delegate what may seem to be a chore. But remember: these notes are going to be the basis of *your* decisions—decisions which you may well be announcing during the meeting. As the leader of the group it's more appropriate (and safer) for you to do the job yourself.

10. **A** Thanking people for their contributions is a pleasant way to end the meeting and fixing a follow-up meeting gives it a business-like edge. Keeping people behind unexpectedly to discuss another topic is *not* recommended.

SCORE 40–50
You are well in control of this most subtle of management skills. Let's hope that your subordinates are learning from your excellent example!

SCORE 20–35
You are probably running your more routine meetings very competently but are less surefooted when the issues are more complicated. Ask an experienced colleague to sit in on one of your more

complex meetings and give you some feedback on your performance.

SCORE 15 or less

You are not really in control of your meetings. Why not talk to your boss or personnel manager about a suitable training course?

---------------TEST 14---------------

Score ONE POINT for each answer which agrees with the following:

1. **A** Making a good speech, like winning a battle, depends upon good preparation. Assessing the audience's level of knowledge is vital since it affects both your objectives and your choice of material.

2. **B** *Never* read your speech (boring) and never leave things to chance (highly risky). Speaking from a few headings will ensure that you sound natural and make your talk 'come alive'.

3. **C** How you begin your presentation is extremely important. Never put yourself down since the audience may agree with you and proceed to go to sleep! Instead, give them a clear route-map of your presentation—an audience is always impressed by a speaker who knows where he is going.

4. **B** It's much safer to ask the people who are sitting furthest away from you. If they can hear you, everyone can!

5. **A** Even if the audience is as technical as you are, it pays to use simple words as much as possible. But for a non-specialist audience you must never try to blind them with science—all that does is to arouse resentment.

6. **B** Never speak at machine-gun speed or painfully slowly: the audience will simply switch off. Vary your speed throughout your talk but always slow down for the really important points.

7. **C** Once again, variety's the word! Try to sound as natural as you do in ordinary conversation and don't be shy about showing your enthusiasm. After all, if *you*

sound bored, you can hardly blame the audience for following your example!

8. **A** You must look at *all* sections of the audience if you want to make a really powerful impact—not talk to the table, the floor, the ceiling or the window! Good eye-contact is essential to an effective presentation.

9. **C** Not to use visuals can be disastrous if you are trying to put across complicated information. Equally, to use them indiscriminately can dilute their impact. A selective approach gives you the best of both worlds.

10. **C** Once you are relaxed and trying to convey your enthusiasm, you will find yourself using gestures as normally as in ordinary conversation with your colleagues and friends. Provided that the gestures are not too flamboyant (and therefore distracting), an audience tends to love a speaker who lets himself go.

11. **C** Unless you are a skilled and confident story-teller, be careful with humour: telling a joke badly can irritate the audience and undermine your self-confidence. Go for the smaller laughs through spontaneous rejoinders to comments and questions.

12. **A** Always finish on a strong note—it's your last chance to influence the audience. A quick summary of some of the major points will reinforce their impact and a final thought-provoking point can often ensure a lively discussion period.

13. **C** Unless you want the audience actually to *use* the handouts during your presentation, it is far better to distribute them at the end of your talk. To provide them at any other time means that at least half the audience will be too busy reading them to listen to you.

SCORE 10–13

You are a very competent speaker who has mastered the techniques of both

preparation and presentation.
SCORE 5–9
There are some gaps in your game.
This test should have helped you to
identify them.
SCORE 4 or less
You have a lot of problems and need
intensive training in speaking techniques. But take heart: with determination and practice you will find that
you will make quite extraordinary
progress.

———————TEST 15———————
Score ONE POINT for every answer
which matches the following:
1. Yes **2.** Yes **3.** Yes **4.** No
5. No **6.** Yes **7.** No **8.** Yes
9. Yes
Questions 10–24: No
Questions 25–40: Yes
SCORE 32–40
You are a highly creative individual
who is always looking for—and trying
out—new approaches. What's more
you encourage your people to challenge established practice and support
them when they run into difficulties.
Your department must be an exciting
place in which to work!
SCORE 21–31
You are by no means uncreative and
have a positive attitude towards new
ideas. Your problem is that you tend
to be over-cautious and a little too
conscious of the risks involved. You
should let yourself go and try following through even apparently wild ideas.
A touch more adventurousness would
yield a bountiful harvest.
SCORE 8–20
Yours must be a very dull group since
you are neither very creative yourself
nor willing to encourage creativity in
others. Try to be less risk-conscious
and develop a more positive outlook
towards your work. Identify some
problem areas. Think of ways of overcoming them. Discuss these ideas with
your people. Consult your colleagues.
If you persevere you'll not only get
more fun out of your job—you'll
transform both your performance and
your image.
SCORE 7 or less
Your company's competitors must be

hoping that there are many more like
you!

———————TEST 16———————
Give yourself TEN POINTS for each
answer that your subordinate agrees
with. N.B. In the case of multi-part
questions, *all* sections must be
answered to win a point.
SCORE 250–300
You know your subordinate very well
indeed and must have a very produc-
tive relationship, based upon mutual
liking and trust.
SCORE 170–240
You know your subordinate quite well
but there are a few interesting aspects
of his background which you have not
discovered. On the whole you have a
pretty good relationship.
SCORE 90–160
You don't know your subordinate
nearly as well as you might. This is
probably because you haven't shown
enough interest in him as an individual. Your relationship is much too
formal and he may well perceive you as
a rather cold fish.
SCORE 80 or less
You are supposed to be managing and
motivating this individual and yet you
scarcely know him! It's hard to see
people rallying around *you* in a crisis if
you persist in being so remote and
insensitive.

———————TEST 17———————
Give yourself THREE POINTS for
each FREQUENTLY and TWO
POINTS for every SOMETIMES.
SCORE 51–60
You are under great strain and need
skilled professional advice to help you
with your problems. Drugs and alcohol are not the answer. Seek help at
once.
SCORE 36–50
You are certainly very run down and
things will get worse unless you take
action *now*. Basically, you need to talk
your problems through with
someone—a psychologist perhaps or
even a trusted friend or colleague.
SCORE 14–35
You are still on the right side of the
border but should guard against your

tendency towards self-pity which is making you vulnerable to quite needless—though as yet not severe—bouts of depression. Count your blessings and try to take a more positive view of your life.

SCORE 13 or less
Like everyone else you have your off days but have learned how to cope with life's occasional storms. So long as you continue to look forward rather than backwards, to be optimistic instead of pessimistic, you will remain happy and content with both your work and your personal life.

---TEST 18---
TEN POINTS for every answer which agrees with the following:

1. **B** As organiser it would be unwise for you to leave the conference venue. Better to leave it to the taxi man.
2. **C** He may object at the time but afterwards he'll bless you for saving his reputation!
3. **B** Never make abrupt movements or try to grab the person—the shock could send him over.
4. **A** Going outside to recruit a replacement would be even more expensive. But don't be caught like this again—identify a possible successor and start training him!
5. **B** Many experienced speakers use this technique. You'll sound more spontaneous and natural than if you use detailed notes.
6. **B** Let him 'talk himself out'—he won't be open to reason until his emotions are exhausted.
7. **C** If his heart is beating, leave it alone. Concentrate on making sure that he can breathe.
8. **C** Your boss would have to be very unfeeling not to respond to such an approach.
9. **B** A friendly discussion in a relaxed atmosphere may persuade her to change her mind. In any event she'll appreciate your thoughtfulness in respecting her feelings.
10. **B** Always turn in the direction of the skid.

SCORE 70–100
You are very confident in a crisis and no doubt inspire confidence in others—the mark of a true leader.
SCORE 40–60
You are like the little girl in the nursery rhyme—when you are good you are very, very good and when you are bad you are horrid! Faced with an emergency, you are just as likely to panic as you are to take charge.
SCORE 30 or less
Any crisis handled by you would probably get worse.

---TEST 19---
SCORE All A's
You are so thoughtful and compassionate that you must be a serious candidate for sainthood! Take care that your overflowing good nature is not exploited by the inefficient and the unscrupulous.
SCORE Mainly A's
You are a highly co-operative person but are by no means a soft touch. You appreciate that life in business, as elsewhere, is a matter of give and take and you do your best to help people who are in a fix. But you would expect such people to do the same for you—and they nearly always do.
SCORE Mainly B's
You are generally very reluctant to inconvenience yourself and tend to try to wriggle out of any situation which could disturb your routine. You are probably seen as a rather self-centred person who isn't really a 'team player' and for whom anything out of the ordinary is either a threat or a nuisance. Don't be surprised if people don't rush to help when *you* have a problem!
SCORE Mainly C's
You must lead a very lonely life!

---TEST 20---
Each answer which matches the following table wins FIVE POINTS:

1. C	2. B	3. B	4. B
5. C	6. A	7. A	8. A
9. B	10. A	11. C	12. B

SCORE 50–60
To use a boxing expression, you certainly know how to 'roll with the punches'! Tough-minded and self-

confident, you are able to deal with crises and setbacks in a quite exemplary manner.

SCORE 30–45

You can generally be relied upon to act positively when things go wrong—it's only occasionally that your emotions get the better of your judgment.

SCORE 15–25

More often than not you react negatively to difficult situations, thereby denying yourself the opportunity of finding creative solutions which will increase your self-esteem. Unless you can change these negative attitudes they will gradually undermine your credibility as a leader.

SCORE 10 or less

Ask not for whom the bell tolls . . . .

TEST 21

Score THREE POINTS for YES, ALWAYS and FREQUENTLY answers and TWO POINTS for OCCASIONALLY or SOMETIMES answers.

SCORE 50–60

Slow down! If you go on like this you will drive your family crazy and ruin your health. A discussion with a psychiatrist might help to give you that sense of proportion which you so badly need.

SCORE 31–49

You are working too hard much too often and risk losing your edge through sheer mental fatigue. Recognise that working to excess is more likely to be seen as a mark of inefficiency than a badge of dedication.

Try to develop more outside interests, spend more time with your family and, above all, force yourself to delegate more work to your subordinates. They are probably grossly underemployed and longing for a chance to prove themselves!

SCORE 11–30

You seem to have achieved a sensible balance between your work and your personal life. You are perfectly capable of pulling out the stops when the occasion demands but in general your efficient self-organisation and working methods enable you to get the best of both worlds.

SCORE 0–10

You are certainly in no danger of collapsing from overwork! You seem to be the archetypal '9–5' employee whose commitment ceases as soon as you leave the office.

TEST 22

Award yourself FIVE POINTS for every YES answer.

SCORE 80–100

No need for you to work excessively long hours or to take work home with you—you are using your time to maximum effect. Bravo!

SCORE 60–75

You are a good time-manager and need to improve in only a few areas which you can probably identify from your test results.

SCORE 30–55

You put a lot of pressure on yourself by your lack of self-discipline in managing your time. Almost certainly your problems lie in three main areas: failure to set priorities, inadequate delegation and inability to cope with distractions such as 'drop-in' visitors. A determined attack on all three fronts would enable you to get much more done in less time.

SCORE 25 or less

You are right on course for a serious health problem or even the sack. Unless you get to grips with your time management you may have all the time in the world to ponder where you went wrong!

TEST 23

Your competitiveness is shown by the number of YES replies.

SCORE 25–30

You are superbly equipped to compete in the toughest of environments. You are either occupying a very senior position or are destined to achieve one.

SCORE 18–24

Basically, you are good promotion material but there are some aspects of your performance where you could display a more competitive spirit. Your results will show you where these areas are and you should get to grips with them immediately if you wish to improve your prospects.

SCORE 8–17

You are only moderately competitive and have probably settled for what you have already achieved. There is nothing wrong with this, provided that you can show that you are still willing to learn and can adapt successfully to changes in your job.

The biggest threat to people in your situation is *complacency*. If you succumb to it, you may quickly find yourself becoming out of date—one of the deadliest of sins for today's executive.

SCORE 7 or less

Perhaps you should be thinking of changing your career?

---TEST 24---

Question:
	1. A 3	2. A 2	3. A 0	4. A 3
	B 2	B 0	B 2	B 2
	C 0	C 3	C 3	C 0
5. A 3	6. A 0	7. A 2	8. A 3
B 0	B 2	B 0	B 0
C 2	C 3	C 3	C 2

SCORE 18–24

You are much too gullible and make easy prey for office politicians and other devious characters who manipulate you to their own advantage.

SCORE 8–17

You are steering a sensible middle course, being neither too trustful nor too suspicious. Life has taught you that things are not always as they seem and that a little caution is sometimes necessary when dealing with sensitive issues.

SCORES 0–7

You are ultra-suspicious and appear to have very little trust in anyone. The trouble is that if you don't show trust you cannot expect to receive it.

---TEST 25---

Give yourself FIVE POINTS for every answer which agrees with the following:

1. **A** Interviewing without a job specification is like trying to navigate without a map: the risk of failure is substantially increased. A good job specification enables you to determine whether the candidate's experience matches the requirements of the job.

2. **A** A few prepared questions covering key areas will serve as an insurance against possible lapses of memory. They will also ensure that you interview each candidate consistently.

3. **B** Showing interest in the candidate's hobbies and interests is an excellent way of relaxing him and of giving him an opportunity to 'find his voice'. Questions about the weather and the traffic are obviously just padding.

4. **B** For the experienced candidate with a substantial track record, questioning him about far-off educational experiences can be a waste of time. This is where you can put your prepared questions to excellent use.

5. **C** If you phrase the question so that the answer is obvious, you learn nothing about the candidate. The ability to ask clear but open-ended questions in a neutral, matter-of-fact tone is perhaps the most subtle and rewarding of all interviewing skills.

6. **B** If you receive an answer which you don't like, remain calm and don't be put off too quickly. Remaining silent will often encourage the candidate to explain his point of view in more detail and, as a result, it may seem more reasonable than at first sight. Following up his original answer with one or two supplementary questions can achieve the same result.

7. **B** Any ambitious candidate is bound to ask this question so prepare for it thoroughly. But be *realistic*—no wild exaggerations or (worst of all) empty assurances about rapid promotion! Outline any studies which the successful candidate will be expected to undertake and give him some real-life examples of people who have progressed from the vacant post to more senior positions.

8. **B** This is sometimes the stage when something really vital emerges which has been missed during

the main part of the interview. Always allow sufficient time for a few final questions—the questions themselves are often revealing about the candidate's interests and motivations.

9. B The things you note are the things you remember. Your notes are also invaluable when you are comparing the merits of the various candidates. *Never* rely solely upon your memory.

10. C The more you talk yourself, the less you will learn about the candidate's experience, his opinions and his judgment. Having created a relaxed atmosphere, let him do the talking—after all, he is the candidate, not you!

SCORE 40–50
You are a crisp, business-like interviewer who prepares well, asks good, clear questions and wastes neither his own nor the candidate's time.

SCORE 20–35
You are not as thorough as you might be and are tending to leave some gaps which an unscrupulous candidate might well exploit. You are probably not preparing for your interviews as carefully as you should and this is making you rather tense and forgetful.

SCORE 0–15
Get yourself some interview training as quickly as possible—your mistakes may be costing your company a good deal of money!

TEST 26

FIVE POINTS for every **A** answer and TWO POINTS for each **B** answer.

SCORE 40–50
You are an excellent ambassador for your company—it should be proud of you! The efforts of public-spirited individuals like you often have far more lasting P.R. value than expensive company publicity campaigns.

SCORE 28–39
You try to help whenever you can, provided that you are not too greatly inconvenienced. In general you have a positive attitude.

SCORE 15–27
You are not totally uncaring but you certainly have to be pushed into doing

anything positive! Try to look upon invitations, requests for help, etc. as an opportunity to increase your company's goodwill. Far from being a nuisance, dealing with them is part of your leadership role.

SCORE 0–14
You are doing your company no favours by being so negative and uncaring in your attitude towards outside activities. People must form a very poor view of your company if your behaviour represents the norm rather than the exception.

TEST 27

Question:	1. A 2	2. A 0	3. A 3	4. A 3
	B 3	B 3	B 2	B 0
	C 0	C 2	C 0	C 2
5. A 0	6. A 3	7. A 0	8. A 3	9. A 2
B 3	B 0	B 2	B 0	B 3
C 2	C 2	C 3	C 2	C 0
10. A 3				
B 2				
C 0				

SCORE 25–30
You should have no major problems in handling consultants since you take great care to observe the two golden rules: select the right consultant and stay in control.

SCORE 16–24
You know what you want from consultants but are occasionally a little over-awed by their 'mystique'. There is no need for you to feel like this since although the consultant may have his specialist skills, *you* are the expert on your own organisation! Nevertheless, you are fully prepared to play a positive role—and that is a crucial requirement for success.

SCORE 8–15
You tend to be a little too passive and to rely too much upon the consultant to carry out tasks which are more properly yours. A successful consultancy assignment is very much a partnership between two professionals: the consultant *and* the client.

It is particularly important that you keep your staff well briefed—without their co-operation the project is almost bound to fail.

SCORE 7 or less
You would be well advised not to use

consultants until you have straightened out your thinking on a number of key issues.

---TEST 28---

FIVE POINTS for each answer which matches the following:

1. C Taking account of any known or likely feelings about your proposal—friendly or hostile—enables you to marshal your arguments in the most effective way and to anticipate possible questions.

2. B A business-like beginning is always welcome. Never risk humour at this vital stage unless the story is relevant, original and you can tell it well.

3. B Always spend sufficient time on exposing the weaknesses of the present situation. You cannot expect people to agree to changes until they are convinced that they are necessary.

4. B Punch home the advantages with as much supporting evidence as you can muster. And don't be afraid to stress how your proposal will benefit the interests of those attending the meeting!

5. B This really is an occasion when 'one picture is worth a thousand words'! An attractive visual—transparency or slide—has much more impact than a handout and gives you better control since you can switch it on or off as you please.

6. C Never compete with a powerful distraction, whether it be a secretary, a low-flying jet or the arrival of coffee. Wait until the distraction is over—if you try to put over important points at such moments you will be wasting your time.

7. B This is your last chance to influence the group so make full use of it! A carefully rehearsed punch-line can make a powerful final impact.

8. A Courtesy and politeness cost nothing and can win you many friends. Interrupting a questioner may strike some members

as brash and cause them to react against your proposal.

9. B Calmness under fire is as impressive in the meeting room as it is on the battlefield. As a result of his astute handling of hostile questions, it is not unknown for a speaker's sternest critics to become his most powerful supporters!

10. A Dealing with the drawbacks of your proposal, honestly and straightforwardly, is an excellent way of establishing your credibility with your audience. But don't go on for too long—they may start losing confidence in your idea!

SCORE 35–50
You can be relied upon to assemble a logical case and to present it imaginatively and enthusiastically.

SCORE 15–30
You are quite capable of structuring and presenting a case but are less confident when dealing with some of the problems which arise during questions and discussion.

SCORE 0–10
If you have colleagues or friends who are in the selling field, try discussing your difficulties with them—after all, they are the professionals. Use this test to identify some specific improvement areas.

---TEST 29---

Give yourself FIVE POINTS for every answer which agrees with the following table. All **B** answers score TWO POINTS.

1. C	**2.** A	**3.** A	**4.** C
5. A	**6.** A	**7.** A	**8.** C
9. C	**10.** C	**11.** C	**12.** C
13. A	**14.** C	**15.** C	**16.** C
17. C	**18.** C	**19.** C	**20.** A

SCORE 80–100
You are in excellent shape—a well-merited reward for your disciplined approach to eating and exercise. Keep up the good work.

SCORE 50–79
You are in pretty good shape and have no serious problems which could interfere with your work. However, it would not take much extra effort for

you to achieve an even higher state of fitness. Use the test to identify where you could make some improvements.

SCORE 25–49

You are probably not in any serious trouble yet but you certainly will be unless you change your life-style. A better diet and, in particular, more exercise would be the best possible investments that you could make in your future.

SCORE 0–24

Have a thorough discussion with your family doctor as soon as possible and heed his advice.

---TEST 30---

Each of the following scores FIVE POINTS:

1. B	2. B	3. B	4. A
5. B	6. A	7. A	8. B
9. B	10. C	11. C	12. C

SCORE 45–60

You are not afraid to speak your mind but you do it in a tactful and constructive manner which generally defuses anger and emotion. Once you have established the facts, you act swiftly and decisively.

SCORE 20–40

You tend to blow hot and cold! Sometimes you get angry and upset and explode with fury; at other times you go to great lengths to avoid an argument. Basically, you lack confidence in your ability to deal with delicate people-problems.

Your best course of action would be to enrol for a course in 'assertiveness training' which would equip you with a number of useful techniques for handling sensitive situations.

SCORE 15 or less

A course on assertiveness could help you too, provided that you are willing to make the effort to change. No doubt about it: your need is great.

---TEST 31---

Score FIVE POINTS for each answer which agrees with the table below:

1. ✓	2. ✗	3. ✗	4. ✓
5. ✓	6. ✓	7. ✗	8. ✓
9. ✗	10. ✗	11. ✓	12. ✗
13. ✓	14. ✗	15. ✓	16. ✓
17. ✗	18. ✓	19. ✓	20. ✓
21. ✓	22. ✓	23. ✗	24. ✗

25. ✓	26. ✓	27. ✓	28. ✓
29. ✓	30. ✓		

SCORE 125–150

A caring, sensitive leader, you win the co-operation of your staff by treating them as individuals. You find great personal satisfaction in helping them to realise their potential and take pride in their achievements. Relaxed and self-confident, you enjoy a high degree of emotional security.

SCORE 80–120

You care a good deal about people and generally manage them in a democratic but highly effective manner, with only the occasional lapse into autocracy. Most people enjoy working with you and find you highly receptive to other points of view.

SCORE 35–75

You are far too suspicious of other people and find it hard to disagree without becoming emotional. You should recognise that trust is a two-way street: to receive it, you have first to give it.

At best, the morale in your group is likely to be patchy, with much grumbling and discontent about the way you handle things. Until you are prepared to treat your staff as responsible adults rather than as mischievous children, you will find many doors locked which ought to be open to you.

SCORE 30 or less

Remember what happened to the dinosaurs?

---TEST 32---

FIVE POINTS for each answer which agrees with the following:

1. B	2. C	3. C	4. C
5. B	6. B	7. A	8. C
9. C	10. C	11. C	12. C

SCORE 50–60

You are a very shrewd politician who knows the importance of coolly evaluating situations and of not rushing into premature or impetuous actions. You have also learned the crucial value of patience and good timing and of keeping a low profile until the right moment arrives.

SCORE 30–45

You are well capable of handling most political situations, with only the occasional touch of abrasiveness—possibly in some aspects of your relations with your boss?

SCORE 15–25

You are a rather rough diamond who probably takes pride in plain speaking. While there are times when bluntness and candour are entirely appropriate, most successful executives use persuasion and subtlety rather than sledgehammer methods. If you are ambitious, you will certainly need to adopt a more flexible style.

SCORE 10 or less

You seem to be a very inflexible person who finds it difficult to handle sensitive situations. Unless you can learn from your mistakes and display greater sure-footedness, it is hard to see you progressing much further. However, if you *do* succeed in changing, you will find that it will benefit you in your personal life as well as in your career.

TEST 33

Each YES answer wins ONE POINT.

SCORE 25–30

You are doing an excellent job of communicating at all of the three key levels: boss, subordinates and colleagues. As a result you inspire confidence, people trust you and there is a first-class team spirit in your group.

SCORE 15–24

You are a good communicator with only a few major improvement areas which you can readily identify from your test results. Start working on these right away: top-flight communicators stand out in any organisation and often become prime candidates for accelerated promotion.

SCORE 6–14

You have some distance to go before you can be considered a good performer in this vital aspect of your job. This is probably the result of an over-cautious, over-secretive attitude towards communication which is bound to damage your image and cause many problems which should never have arisen.

Remember: it is the responsibility of those who have information to pass it on to those who need it—*not* the responsibility of those who need it to

fight tooth and nail to get it! So relax—and start communicating! This is what good leadership is all about.

SCORE 5 or less

Have you taken a vow of silence? This really is an appalling score which seems to indicate that you would be happier working in a 'lone wolf' role rather than one which requires you to lead and motivate people.

TEST 34

Score ONE POINT for every affirmative answer.

SCORE 13–15

You are doing all the right things and, with continuing good performance in your job, you should be extremely well-placed to achieve your goal.

SCORE 8–12

You are taking several positive steps to improve your prospects. However, take another look at your personal training needs—it could be that there are some gaps here which need filling.

SCORE 3–7

You have a great deal to do before you can be considered a really serious promotion contender. It's not too late to catch up but you need to devise a much more positive strategy—and quickly.

SCORE 2 or less

You are not really ambitious at all—or, if you are, you are not prepared to do much about it.

TEST 35

Questions 1–3: FIVE POINTS for **A** answers, THREE POINTS for **B** answers.

Questions 4–10: FIVE POINTS for every answer which agrees with the following:

4. A	5. B	6. B
7. C	8. C	9. A
10. B		

SCORE 39–50

You read widely and systematically and are most unlikely to be caught napping by new developments and techniques. Are you encouraging your subordinates to follow your excellent example?

SCORE 30–38

You are quite well read, particularly in terms of business journals, but now need to include a few more high-quality books in your reading schedule. Some of those mentioned in the test could provide you with a useful springboard.

SCORE 14–29

You clearly haven't realised how close you are to being regarded by your colleagues and (worse still) your boss as outdated and 'over the hill'. You will need to move fast if you are to retain your credibility.

SCORE 0–13

If your family doctor read as little about medicine as you read about management, you would have every right to feel dubious about taking his advice. Your boss probably feels the same way about you.

TEST 36

Score ONE POINT for every YES answer.

SCORE 22–30

You have so many interests that it's amazing that you can find the time to stagger into work! Aren't you overdoing it a little? Take care that your outside activities do not begin to affect your commitment to your job.

SCORE 13–21

You are leading a very full and balanced life, with a wide range of interests which keep you both physically fit and mentally active. Given so many stimulating pursuits, you are unlikely to lose your sharpness at work—indeed you should be extremely well-placed to progress further in your career.

SCORE 6–12

There is plenty of scope for you to spread your wings and get much more involved in non-business activities. Every executive needs a period of recreation—a change of pace with new faces and new places to add colour and variety to his life. By broadening your interests you will not only enjoy life more: you will be investing in your future success.

SCORE 5 or less

You are leading a very humdrum life which, unless you change it, could lead to you losing your edge at work. You owe it to yourself to get more fun out of life. Act *now*.

TEST 37

Give yourself FIVE POINTS for each of the following:

1. C	2. B	3. C	4. B
5. B	6. A	7. A	8. B
9. A	10. B		

SCORE 40–50

You are a very mature person whose ego and emotions are well under control, without this in any way weakening the strength of your convictions.

SCORE 20–35

While you generally take care not to display your feelings in an unacceptable manner, you are not as tolerant as you might be. At times you have a tendency to bottle things up and to look for opportunities to 'level the score' at a later date.

SCORE 0–15

You are very intolerant of opinions and behaviour which differ from your own and are liable to express your disagreements in a way that turns people against you. Be careful that you are not labelled as a bigot—in an age of change that could be quite a handicap!

TEST 38

Score FIVE POINTS for every YES answer.

SCORE 150–170

You write in a clear, concise style which leaves little scope for ambiguity or misunderstanding—a talent which is no doubt much appreciated by your readers.

SCORE 100–145

You have no serious problems but your writing would benefit if you were to adopt a slightly more relaxed style, with rather fewer concessions to 'traditional' practices. Check, too, whether there are any improvements which you could make in such areas as preparation and structure.

SCORE 50–95

Your writing is far too formal and ponderous and is more likely to confuse than to clarify. Your test results will spotlight your priority needs but, above all, you need to change your *attitude* to writing.

Imagine yourself *talking* to your readers instead of writing to them and remember the golden rules: have a clear aim and use simple, natural words. Persevere with these 'basics' of good writing and many of your problems will melt away.

SCORE 45 or less
In the interests of your readers' blood-pressure, write only as a last resort.

---TEST 39---

Question:

	1.	2.	3.	4.
	A 5	A 0	A 0	A 2
	B 2	B 5	B 2	B 0
	C 0	C 2	C 5	C 5

	5.	6.	7.	8.	9.
	A 2	A 0	A 5	A 0	A 5
	B 0	B 2	B 0	B 2	B 0
	C 5	C 5	C 2	C 5	C 2

	10.
	A 0
	B 2
	C 5

SCORE 40–50
Your self-confidence is quite extraordinary and you appear to thrive on challenge and excitement. You could well be more suited to running your own business than working as an employee.

SCORE 15–39
You cope very comfortably with most of the challenges you meet and only draw back occasionally from high-risk situations.

SCORE 14 or less
You have little taste for risk or excitement and invariably attempt to 'play it safe'. Are you *sure* that you are suited to a business career?

---TEST 40---

The more questions you can answer with a 'YES' the greater the individual's potential. ONE POINT for each affirmative.

SCORE 30–35
A very good prospect indeed. An individual of this calibre must be promoted quickly or he may well decide to seek pastures new.

SCORE 21–29
Clearly a person of considerable potential but with a number of areas where some improvement is possible. Concentrate your coaching efforts on these areas and encourage him to undertake some self-development activities.

SCORE 11–20
It looks as though you may have exaggerated this person's potential—probably by over-rating one or two of his strengths. He has a good deal to do before he can be realistically considered for a significant promotion. Identify his priority needs and seek the help of your personnel or training manager in developing an improvement plan.

SCORE 10 or less
Think again.

---TEST 41---

Award yourself FIVE POINTS for every YES answer.

SCORE 65–75
No one working for you should have the slightest doubt about what is expected of him. If your leadership skills match your ability to set objectives, you must be running a thoroughly professional operation with plenty of job satisfaction for everyone involved.

SCORE 40–60
You are on the right lines but may need to pay more attention to one or two specific areas, such as getting your subordinates fully involved in objective-setting (see Questions 12–15). Employees tend to be much more enthusiastic about achieving objectives which have been discussed with them than those which have been imposed.

SCORE 15–35
Your objective-setting is not nearly as thorough as it should be and there is probably a good deal of confusion and misunderstanding among your people about what you expect of them. Use the test results as a checklist and start right away on plugging the gaps.

SCORE 10 or less
Your people must be wandering around in a kind of fog, desperately trying to find out what they are supposed to be doing. Consider yourself lucky to be holding your job … but for how much longer?

---TEST 42---

Question 1 : A = 1 point
Questions 2–8 : B = 1 point
Questions 9–15: A = 1 point

SCORE 12–15
You work very hard at getting the message—and nearly always do. What's more, most people enjoy talking to you: they are flattered by your interest and attention.

SCORE 6–11

You are reasonably attentive if the subject interests you but are rather easily distracted by minor factors. Recognise that listening is like any other skill—you need constant practice and a lot of determination. One lapse of concentration can sometimes cost you dearly.

SCORE 5 or less

Anyone who is as poor a listener as you is bound to make mistakes—and infuriate those who try to communicate with you.

Be warned: poor listeners are often thought of as being either arrogant or stupid—sometimes both!

TEST 43

Clearly the factors marked 'IMPORTANT' are the ones which matter to you.

Group A

If most of them occur between Questions 1 and 15, then you work best in a congenial working environment, in a job which you find moderately interesting and not too demanding and in a paternalistic organisation which 'looks after you' in terms of fringe benefits and employee facilities. You value stability and predictability more than adventure and excitement since you are very conscious of the risks that go with failure.

It is likely that you find your true satisfaction outside your work in the shape of sporting, social or cultural interests or perhaps in an absorbing hobby. You are likely to find great satisfaction in your family life.

Group B

If most of your 'IMPORTANT' factors occur between Questions 16 and 30, you are an ambitious, competitive individual who works best in a demanding job with plenty of variety. You enjoy working under pressure and thrive upon opportunities to use your initiative. You dislike being closely supervised or having to conform to a plethora of rules and regulations. You expect to be rewarded according to your results and are constantly on the look-out for promotion opportunities.

It is unlikely that you have any particularly strong interests outside your job, though you may be a keen golfer—a game which you see largely as providing opportunities to generate business contacts.

Group C

If your 'IMPORTANT' factors are fairly evenly distributed between both groups of questions, then you are neither a 'safety first' person nor an out-and-out go-getter. You like your work and enjoy a challenge but you are not prepared to sacrifice your family or personal interests to claw your way to the top.

You enjoy responsibility and decision-making and expect to be recognised for good performance. But you are by no means ultra-ambitious and whilst anxious to avoid becoming bored in your work, you would think very carefully before accepting any assignment with a high degree of risk.

Basically you are what most organisations regard as the salt of the earth—a solid, reliable performer who takes pride in his work and feels a strong sense of personal loyalty to the organisation which employs him.

TEST 44

If your answers consist mainly of **A** choices, you are a strong, dominant personality who enjoys leading from the front and acting decisively. You always give priority to getting the job done, believing that people should be prepared to subordinate their interests to this overriding goal. You are a demanding taskmaster who insists upon high standards of performance and you have tremendous energy and zest for work. You are rather uncomfortable with situations which require you to consult your subordinates, believing that 'managers must manage' and that too much participation slows down decision-making. Greatly respected for your leadership and drive, you can sometimes inspire fear among those who work for you.

If your answers consist mainly of **B** choices, you are a very people-oriented executive who believes that teamwork and good inter-personal relationships are the key factors in achieving results. A keen practitioner of participative methods of decision-making, you see yourself as a coach and developer of people rather than a source of direction and control. In your concern for individuals, you sometimes overlook the needs of the business and this could affect your promotion prospects. You are well-liked by your staff but are not always as respected as much as you think you are—sometimes they yearn for you to act more quickly and decisively!

If your answers consist mainly of C choices, you are a pragmatic, down-to-earth executive who tends to judge both individuals and situations strictly on their merits. You see yourself (and are generally seen by others) as a practical man who gets results by common-sense and sheer 'nous' and you tend to be dismissive of 'airy-fairy' theories about human behaviour and management style. Your great strength is your ability to act decisively whilst at the same time getting people to co-operate with you. From the point of view of higher management you are perceived as a most capable executive with a mature and balanced outlook. Their main reservations are whether you are sufficiently responsive to change and whether you can think strategically as well as tactically.

TEST 45

Question:	1. A 0	2. A 0	3. A 0	4. A 3
	B 2	B 3	B 3	B 2
	C 3	C 2	C 2	C 0
5. A 3	6. A 2	7. A 2	8. A 2	9. A 0
B 2	B 0	B 3	B 3	B 3
C 0	C 3	C 0	C 0	C 2
10. A 3	B 0	C 2		

SCORE 24–30
You become far too emotional when the pressure is on. Behaviour which to you may seem justifiably forceful may to others appear brash and bullying.
SCORE 14–23
You are a strong personality who enjoys getting his own way and generally do so without being offensive. You are seen as a 'toughie' who doesn't suffer fools gladly but people respect you for your honesty and sincerity.
SCORE 7–13
You are much too reluctant to stand

up for yourself. Unless you can acquire greater self-confidence it is hard to see you being selected for any role requiring forceful leadership and the ability to take unpopular decisions.
SCORE 0–6
You are far too easily brushed aside. Being so self-effacing may be saintly but in business it can be suicidal.

TEST 46

Award yourself ONE POINT for every answer which matches the following:
1. Yes 2. Yes 3. Yes 4. Yes
5. No 6. Yes 7. Yes 8. Yes
9. Yes 10. Yes 11. No 12. No
13. No 14. Yes 15. Yes 16. Yes
17. No 18. No 19. No 20. Yes
21. No 22. Yes
SCORE 17–22
You are very much at ease at all kinds of social events and clearly relish the challenge of meeting new people. Your friendly manner and lack of pomposity, together with your genuine interest in other people, makes you a popular figure at company social functions and an excellent ambassador at non-company events.
SCORE 11–16
You cope perfectly well with most social events, though you are perhaps slightly more at ease with people you know well. Your test results indicate that there are a few situations where you need more self-confidence and you should now concentrate upon improving in these specific areas.
SCORE 5–10
Whether as a result of shyness, lack of small talk or disinterest in others, you are sadly lacking in self-confidence. At times when you should be relaxed and convivial, you probably feel under considerable strain.

If you are going to feel more at ease, you must change your self-image. Think of yourself as an interesting person who does an interesting job and leads an interesting life. Look upon others as equally interesting people with whom you can exchange ideas and experiences and from whom you may possibly learn something of value.

SCORE 4 or less
You are clearly a loner who dislikes socialising of any kind. You are probably perceived as somewhat eccentric.

───────────TEST 47───────────
Each YES answer wins FIVE POINTS.
SCORE 125–150
You are a highly efficient executive who thinks deeply about each of the key areas of his job and develops clear-cut plans to achieve his objectives. You are setting a superb example to your staff and are no doubt highly regarded both by your peers and top management.

SCORE 80–120
You are a very reliable and efficient performer with few significant shortcomings and a great many more strengths. Examine your test results carefully to see whether your weaknesses are clustered in any particular area (e.g. developing individuals) and go all-out to eliminate them.

SCORE 35–75
You are not fully in control of your job, probably because you are not thinking broadly enough over the full range of your responsibilities. For example, concentrating exclusively on 'the job' itself and neglecting to develop individuals or encourage team spirit can lead to many unnecessary problems and self-inflicted wounds.

As a result of such imbalances in performance, many executives acquire a reputation for inefficiency. Act now before you join them!

SCORE 30 or less
For your subordinates' sake, let's hope that you are not too far off retirement!

───────────TEST 48───────────
Give yourself THREE POINTS for each YES, ALWAYS and FREQUENTLY answer and TWO POINTS for every OCCASIONALLY or SOMETIMES answer.
SCORE 51–60
You are far too aggressive and seem prepared to ride roughshod over everyone to get your own way. Such ruthlessness can only damage your career prospects—people nowadays expect to be led by someone they can

trust and respect, not by an overgrown school bully.
SCORE 36–50
Occasionally, when under severe pressure, you can 'go over the top' and behave in a manner which you may later regret. On the whole, however, you are seen as a 'tough guy' who is firm but fair.

SCORE 14–35
You are a little too easy-going and are often reluctant to assert yourself in situations where people may be looking to you for a lead. You would probably benefit from some training in leadership skills which would help you to deal with the kind of situations which you are at present avoiding.

SCORE 13 or less
You seem to be a human doormat, content to allow people to walk all over you. Unless you pull yourself together and begin acting like a leader, your own survival prospects may be at risk.

───────────TEST 49───────────
Score THREE POINTS for every NEVER answer and ONE POINT for every SOMETIMES.
SCORE 50–60
You have an excellent memory which rarely lets you down. Your ability to recall personal as well as business information is most impressive and reinforces your image as a caring, efficient executive.

SCORE 36–49
You have a good memory and it's unusual for you to forget anything important. Occasionally you come unstuck on minor things, probably because your mind is on weightier matters.

SCORE 16–35
You frequently forget things, both major and minor, and this sometimes gives the impression that you are not on top of your job. It can also result in people feeling hurt and resentful.

To strengthen your memory, make full use of simple memory aids such as your diary, 'post-it' notes and a desk calendar on which you can ring any important dates. Make sure, too, that you have a good 'bring forward' system.

SCORE 15 or less

Your memory is certainly in poor shape and you need to take drastic action to get it working properly again. In addition to following the above advice, you would probably benefit from a course in Pelmanism.

————TEST 50————

Questions 1–30 : FIVE POINTS for every YES.
Questions 31–40: FIVE POINTS for every NO.

SCORE 160–200

You are satisfied with both your job and your career—and are loyal to your employer too. You find your job challenging and fulfilling and have lost none of your enthusiasm for a career which has provided an excellent vehicle for your talents.

SCORE 105–155

While you get quite a lot of satisfaction from your job and have almost certainly chosen the right career, there are a number of factors in your present situation which irritate you or cause you to feel frustrated.

These may only be temporary—every executive goes through the occasional bad patch. However, should they begin to build up and to affect your performance, perhaps you should consider changing your employer.

SCORE 60–100

You are very dissatisfied in your present job and may not be well suited to your career. Your chances of making a fresh start will, of course, depend largely upon your age, qualifications and domestic situation. Nevertheless, if you are both marketable and mobile, you should at least consider making a change. The longer you leave it, the more your current job will seem like a prison sentence.

SCORE 55 and below

You really are in a most unhappy state, with little satisfaction from any aspect of your working life. If you have an opportunity to do something more congenial, seize it with both hands. If not, then develop a wide range of interests outside your work to provide you with the stimulation which is so lacking in your job.